God Is
My Witnes

Feb '83
Frances Wragg

God Is My Witness

THE STORY OF THE WORLD-FAMOUS HEALER

E. G. Fricker

EYRE & SPOTTISWOODE (Publishers) LTD
LONDON

First published in Great Britain
by Arthur Barker Limited
This edition first published 1979
by Eyre & Spottiswoode (Publishers) Ltd
11 New Fetter Lane, London EC4P 4EE

ISBN 0 413 80030 X

Printed in Great Britain by
Richard Clay (The Chaucer Press) Ltd
Bungay, Suffolk

Contents

Why?

Please tell me, Lord, the answer to the question why
You put us on this Earth, to live a little day, and then to die?
We are born into this world—the fruit of Love and Pain
and live in suffering till 'tis time to leave again.
Alone we come. Alone we walk through Life. Alone we go.
And yet the purpose of it all we do not know.

—Anonymous

Prologue

This is a story about two worlds.

Whatever you may think, this world that we see about us is not the only one. If you find this hard to believe, it is not surprising; it never occurred to me either that after we leave this world we continue life instantaneously in another, until one memorable day over twenty-five years ago when I received such convincing proof that I could no longer doubt.

Indeed I have already been to that other world and have been shown the very house where I am to live after I have finally left this world in the natural way.

But more about that later.

Not only that, but I talk daily with doctors and spirit people in the other world who help me with my work of healing the sick.

As I have, as it were, one foot in both worlds, perhaps you may think that I have an unfair advantage. But to even things up a little, I would like to share some of my experiences with you so that your doubts may turn to certainty about those things I *know* to be true.

I can understand so well the loneliness of those nearing the end of their journey in this world who are fearful of what is going to happen to them, and the hopelessness of those who can see nothing for themselves but the total extinction of mind and body.

My greatest wish is that these words may reach the hearts of all such sufferers and bring them comfort in their distress.

Perhaps when you have read the last page of this book you, too, may become convinced, as I was.

Who knows?

God Is My Witness

1

A Voice from the Other World

The story begins in *this* world, when I first saw the light of a March day in Highgate in the year 1910.

This was no new experience for my parents, as I was the seventh of eight sons, not to mention three daughters, two of whom, unhappily, died before I was born.

My parents were wonderful people, my father being a printer who was able very successfully to support his not inconsiderable family. My mother, to whom I was very close, was a Quaker. She was an excellent cook—she had to be with a family of that size—and she taught me everything she knew about it, which in later life stood me in very good stead and has remained one of my interests to this day.

One day when I was about five years old I heard a Voice talking to me, which was very puzzling as I could see nobody there. Day after day this Voice would tell me all sorts of marvelous things and would give me constant and friendly advice. For instance, if I were going somewhere, the Voice would say, "No, you must not go that way. Go the other!"

Whether it was to prevent my being killed or something of that kind I do not know, but it must have been very persuasive because I always heeded the warnings. At first I felt rather frightened, as any child would be. All the time I used to hear this Voice telling me things that filled we with wonder, until at last I accepted it as the Voice of a friend, albeit with authority which I respected as much as that of my parents.

When I first heard it, naturally I wanted to talk about it to my mother. But every time I attempted to tell her, the Voice used to say to me, "You must not tell your parents or anyone else about this. We have sent so many people since man has been on earth, and always they have been crucified, burned, or sent to an asylum because they could hear a Voice. People do not realize what it is all about, so you must keep this to yourself at all times. We know it will be difficult for you, but we will help you by giving you a warning if you should attempt to tell someone."

Not fancying the idea of such an unpleasant fate, I maintained a prudent silence on the subject. But it was not at all easy.

I went to an elementary school in the usual way, and I remember asking some of my friends if they ever heard a Voice when there was nobody there. They just laughed at the time, but when I was older and asked them the same question, they hinted darkly that I needed my head examined. This so shocked me that I never brought the subject up again.

But in spite of this incident I did not feel in the least isolated from other children, and my consolation for keeping the secret was that my Voice told me such wonderful things.

At first when my Voice spoke to me I used to carry on conversations aloud, but as this was impossible in the presence of other people, I soon learned to converse mentally.

Sometimes my Voice told me that certain things were going to happen, and they always did.

On one occasion my Voice told me that my Aunt Martha was coming to see us. Without thinking, I said to my mother, "Aunt Martha is coming to see us soon, Mum."

She looked at me and said, "What *are* you talking about? That's impossible. I haven't seen her for about twelve years!"

"I'm sorry," I mumbled, regretting my slip, "I must have made a mistake."

No sooner had I uttered these words than there was a knock on the door. It was Aunt Martha!

"Oh dear!" I thought, "that's done it!"

"You just told me she was coming," said my mother with a puzzled expression. "How on earth did you know? I suppose it was just a guess."

"Yes," I answered, relieved at being offered this way to escape from my indiscretion. "I reckon I just guessed it."

I had received a basic religious training from my mother, and as time went on I explained to myself that my Voice must be the Voice of God. My Voice gave me guidance and helped me to solve my problems and everything it said to me was invariably correct, so from where else could it come?

It was most useful when my mother sent me out to do the shopping. My Voice would say, "You will not find what you want in that shop, go on to the next one." And, sure enough, I would find what I was looking for, much to the surprise of my mother, who had not been able to find it herself.

These incidents may seem trifling in themselves, but I can now see that they were designed to convince me that I could trust my Voice implicitly.

At that time it never dawned on me that there is another life in another world after death. Perhaps I was not meant to know until much later, when I learned of my healing mission.

I accepted my Voice as the Voice of God, which I still do to this day, but in the light of experience I realize that it probably is conveyed to me by one of God's many servants in the other world.

Be that as it may, I obey my Voice today without question in the same way I used to do as a child.

I enjoyed my life at school, and for some reason my friends often brought me their problems, with which I used to help. Frequently these problems were financial, and my Voice would urge me to hand over a sixpence, which always gave me a warm satisfaction. It was all part of my training to give help and love to everybody.

I enjoyed mixing freely with people of all classes and creeds, and when I was about thirteen this led me to ask my parents if I could do a job in my spare time.

I have always loved flowers, and my mother suggested that I should go to the flower market with a hired barrow and sell flowers in the street. I thought this was a splendid idea, and I used to go off to Covent Garden at six in the morning and load up my barrow with flowers. In this way I met a lot of different people, and my friends would come and chat with me. As often as not, they would bring their problems to me for advice, and with the help of my Voice I was able to solve them.

After a time I decided to set up a sweet stall, which attracted more young people. I worked all day on Saturdays and every night as well. By adding ice cream to my wares, I managed to increase my custom enormously. Nothing gave me greater pleasure than to be able to give one of my friends a present of a packet of sweets out of the profits.

At the age of fourteen I left school and devoted my time entirely to my sweet stall. My father wanted me to follow in his footsteps and become a printer, but this was easier said than done.

He put forward my name to the father of the chapel of printers in Islington. I could not become an apprentice until I had been accepted by the chapel, and I was instructed to report there every day until such time as they decided to accept me.

This daily pilgrimage continued for a year, and always the answer was the same: "Not today, lad!"

My patience was running out, and by this time I was getting bored with my sweet stall. I wanted a proper job so that I could give my mother money out of my wages just as my brothers did. My mother refused to accept any of the proceeds from my sweet stall, treating it merely as a source of pocket money for me.

My brothers were all butchers and they seemed to find the job good fun, and I felt that I wanted to be a butcher like them. By this time I was fifteen, but I had not yet grown very much. A butcher's work was sometimes heavy, and as I had suffered a great deal of illness during my childhood, I was not strong.

One day I was walking down Seven Sisters Road when I saw in the window of a shoe shop an advertisement inviting applications for one vacant job. Rather diffidently I entered the shop and encountered the manageress, who told me to come back at two as there were other applicants to be interviewed. When I returned, I found a long queue of lads towering over me, and I did not much fancy my chances. However, I tacked myself onto the end of the line, and, when my turn came, I was amazed when the manageress told me that I had got the job. She wanted me to start there and then, but I had to clear up my sweet stall, so I said that I would come the next morning.

Although I was proud to think that I had at last got my first job, it proved not to be as exciting as I had hoped, my duties consisting of cleaning up the place and being generally at everybody's beck and call. So I decided to ask one of the staff how I could raise myself from this boring and menial position. I was told that in order to become an assistant I would have to learn all the numbers on the shoe boxes corresponding to the different sizes, of which there seemed to be hundreds. Nothing daunted, I set to work to learn them by heart, and for some time I never even went out to lunch.

After about two months one of the assistants left, and I asked for the job. The manageress said she would try me out, and I felt I had at last got my foot on the first rung of the ladder.

But my enthusiasm was short-lived, for it seemed that I had jumped out of the frying pan into the fire.

Some customers would try dozens of pairs of shoes, whose numbers I had so arduously learned, only to say at the end that they would think about it and come back next week. This used to make me furious, and many were the occasions when inwardly I muttered some of those colorful expletives which I had unfortunately picked up during my Covent Garden days. So much was I affected by these constant annoyances that I used to give vent to my feelings by calling out terrible imprecations in my sleep upon the heads of my customers, until finally my mother insisted that I leave the job.

However, my knowledge of human nature had expanded.

If you want something enough, it very often turns up, and one day I saw an advertisement for a roundsman in a butcher's shop. This was the opportunity for which I had been waiting, and I jumped at the chance. On the same day that I was due to start work at the butcher's shop, a letter arrived from the printer's chapel offering to take me as an apprentice. My father naturally wanted me to take the apprenticeship, but I insisted that I had already promised to work for the butcher. After some family discussion and a little help from my mother it was agreed that I should take the job of butcher's roundsman. It was the sort of thing I enjoyed doing because it meant that I had to go out delivering orders and in this way I was able to meet all sorts of people. For some reason they used to tell me their problems, and always my Voice would help me to provide the right solutions.

I was happy and settled in my work until one day I was struck down by rheumatic fever, which was the beginning of a period of almost continual illness. I learned the meaning of pain during this serious disease through which my mother nursed me with loving care. Anyone who has had rheumatic fever will know what suffering it can cause. I feel sure that at this time my mother was helped from the other world by thoughts put into her mind about how I should be treated, for I recovered without any lasting damage which can so often result from this complaint.

I went back to my work, which often entailed lifting quite heavy loads. Although I had grown by this time, it proved too much for my strength and I developed a hernia. I had to go into the hospital for an operation, and I remember one morning saying to my neighbor in the next bed, "I wish to goodness this operation was over!"

"Don't be silly," he answered, "you've just had it!"

Unbelievingly, I tried to sit up, and the excruciating pain convinced me that he was telling the truth!

By a strange coincidence, a fortnight after I was discharged, my father had exactly the same trouble, and not only was he sent to the same hospital, but he was put into the same ward and into the identical bed which I had just vacated! Nobody, in fact, realized that he was my father, but when I went to visit him I had great fun seeing my old friends and the nurses who had looked after me.

Some weeks after my operation I began to have the most terrible pains, but when I went back to the hospital I was told it was just the result of the operation and that it would subside. It did nothing of the sort, and six times I went to different hospitals for advice, only to be told the same thing and that the best remedy was to take walking exercise. Finally I collapsed, and I knew that if something was not done I would die.

At this point my Voice intervened and told me that I must go at once to a German hospital. I did not know that a German hospital even existed, but in obedience to my Voice I consulted the doctor once more. After being told that nothing more could be done for me, I mentioned to the doctor that I wanted to go to a German hospital. After much persuasion he gave me a letter to a German hospital which turned out to be quite near my home.

I must say that they were most efficient, and after a series of tests I was told that I must stay in the hospital for an immediate operation for peritonitis. Otherwise, I should die. At my request they got in touch with my mother, and there and then I was placed on a cart and taken into the operating theater. On the way I was not greatly encouraged by the nurse asking me which was my nearest police station so that my parents could be informed if anything should go wrong!

The whole business was most efficient but quite terrifying; I was given only a local anesthetic in the spine and legs, so that I was numb from the waist downward. Two nurses held my hands partly for comfort and partly for restraint, and I was told not to look into the mirrors of the operating lamp. Of course I could not keep my eyes away, and, to my horror, I was able to see my stomach being cut open. Needless to say, I fainted with shock, which was perhaps just as well.

It was then that I had a very strange experience which I have never forgotten.

I felt that I was out of my body and found myself walking up a beautiful white-marble staircase with a balustrade on each side. In brilliant sunshine the marble was snow-white and glistening, and the staircase disappeared into the distance so that I could not see where it was leading. I heard the murmur of a thousand voices, but as I hurriedly climbed the steps to find out from where they came, I could not see anybody. Continuing my ascent of the staircase, I distinctly heard a voice calling to me, "Come back! Come back!"

I must then have returned to my body, for when I opened my eyes I saw the German doctor bending over me gripping my cheeks and shaking me to bring me back to consciousness. Whether it was his voice that I had heard I do not know. This was my first experience of that "other" world, which even then I still did not realize existed. Perhaps this experience was meant to show me that the spirit is whole and preserved from harm when it is out of the body—even during an operation—but at the time it meant nothing to me.

I can see now that these experiences were all part of my training for my mission of healing. Out of them grew an understanding and sympathy for the sick, and through my own suffering the desire was born to help them and alleviate their pain.

Although at this time I knew nothing of healing power, I can discern the pattern of my life developing always toward this purpose, which was not fulfilled until twenty years later.

After I had fully recovered from the operation, my

health improved and I had no further serious illness. I was then about twenty years old, and I continued to work as a butcher, making steady progress in periodic promotions. When I was twenty-five I married my wife, Grace, and in 1938 my son, Derek, was born, followed in 1942 by my daughter Rita and later by my younger daughter, Theresa, in 1948.

Just before World War II, I had reached the position of manager of the butcher's business, but I had to give up my job when I was called up into the forces at the outbreak of hostilities. I served in the army for six years.

I can recall very clearly going for my medical inspection. There were two men in front of me, and the doctor asked the first one if he had had rheumatic fever. He replied that he most certainly had and it had lasted for a month. The doctor passed him immediately as fit and then asked the second man the same question. He also said that he had had rheumatic fever and raised the period to six weeks. Again the doctor had no hesitation in passing him as fit.

When it came to my turn and I was asked the same question, I was so embarrassed that I said I had never had the illness. I wanted to join the army, and I was afraid that in my case the doctor might believe me. Thus I was enrolled.

Soon after the beginning of the war, my wife and son, Derek, were evacuated from London, and I used to spend my short leaves at the house of my parents. Unhappily my mother had contracted cancer about six months after the outbreak, and she became very seriously ill. The last time I saw her was on one of these short leaves in 1941.

She was suffering terrible pain, and I sat up with her all night. Although there was clearly nothing I could do beyond comforting her with my love, she kept on saying to me, "Ted, put your hands on me. You can cure me." I did not understand what she meant, and I dared not touch her for fear of hurting her. But to comfort her I held both her hands in mine until at last she grew quieter and the pain seemed easier.

It is possible that my mother was at times out of her body and had been told to say this to me. Perhaps her time to leave this world had come, and she was, in fact, beyond help except for the comfort and relief from pain which I was allowed to give her.

At that moment my Voice kept silent, but later I was advised that my mother's doctor should be changed.

I mentioned this to my sister, who was of the same mind, and from then onward my mother was looked after by an African doctor who was able to do much to relieve her pain. She died just before Christmas 1941.

It was sad that I was not able to heal my own mother, but since then I have made up for it by healing many other people's mothers.

My father lived on until 1950. He was a happy soul, and when his time was about to come I went to see him. He had periods of unconsciousness when he was out of his body, and he would come back and joke that he had a few hours left yet. Finally he passed peacefully away.

After my enrollment in the army, I found my mother's early training in cookery very useful, and I joined the army catering corps where I became a catering adviser in a very short time as I had a head start over the others, having been brought up to it.

I am very fond of cooking—in fact, I almost prefer it to eating—because it is a creative activity which is full of continuous interest.

I was made a sergeant and then, soon afterward, was offered a commission in the rank of captain, which I refused. Everyone thought I was stupid not to accept it, but I thought differently. In my heart I wanted to accept, but I could not do so because I felt it would deprive me of the companionship of the ordinary rank and file. If I were to become an officer, I felt, it would be impossible to talk to the ordinary chaps in quite the same way as before, whereas as a sergeant I could mix and talk with them and at the same time I could talk freely to the officers.

I think I was guided to the right decision because, by keeping touch in this way, I was able to help quite a number of them and make them a little happier than they would otherwise have been under the war conditions.

All this time my Voice continued to give me advice, and I was told that I must try to help my companions, many of whom were miserably homesick when they first joined up. I used to try to cheer them up by organizing singsongs and similar activities, and many of them brought me their problems, to which I was able to give solutions with the advice of my Voice. To those who were scared as we took part in the invasion of Normandy, I used to say that if we were going to be killed we might as well die happy. This made them laugh and dispersed their fears.

After the invasion of Normandy we went right on through into Germany. I remember on one occasion, as we were traveling in a convey of lorries into Germany after the crossing of the Rhine, I saw a German boy about eight years old and his little sister aged about four. She was clinging to him, obviously scared of what must have seemed to her those horrid foreign soldiers. I was sitting on a pile of rations, so I reached behind me and grabbed a big handful of chocolate which I threw to the two little children in order to show them that our intentions were not hostile. We passed by so quickly that there was no time to see the result, but I like to think that it comforted them a little.

In January 1946 I was demobilized at a place called Wuppertal, near Düsseldorf. I returned home from there on leave to find that my previous experience in the meat trade was now of little use, since meat was, of course, still rationed. So I said to my wife, "Well, it looks as though I shall have to start all over again at something else if I'm going to make a living."

One day I was sitting thinking about all this when my Voice said to me, "Now look! If you are going to start in a completely new type of business, there is only one way in which you will be successful, and that is that you must go into a job as a manager."

Looking back on it now, it was not so silly as it sounded to me then. After all, I had been manager of a business before the war, and during my army life I had had a great deal of experience in organization and also in the management of men.

However, at the time it seemed to me a great joke, but as usual I did what my Voice said.

I was told to look in the newspapers and write for any job that took my fancy. I had nothing to lose, I told myself, for if they were not satisfied with me after a month, all I could get was the sack.

I answered advertisement after advertisement until one day I got a reply. The job offered me was as manager of a factory, but there was no mention of what the factory was making.

"Well!" I thought to myself, "it doesn't matter much what they make, I can still organize things and I know how to deal with men."

So, with some misgivings, off I went and was interviewed by the owner, who told me that during the war his business had suffered a great deal and that he wanted someone to put in charge who would be able to increase production. The factory produced mirrors and fancy glass of all kinds.

"Well," he said to me after the interview, "I have two other chaps to see, but I'll send you a telegram by this evening to tell you if you've got the job or not. But I think you have a fair chance."

Six o'clock came that evening and there was no news. I thought, "I must have lost that job. Perhaps I was too big-headed or something."

Funnily enough, it was my birthday and I was going to take my wife out to dinner. Just as we were going out of the door a boy arrived with a telegram. All it said was: "Report on Monday." It nearly shook the life out of me, as I wondered what I had let myself in for. However, as you can imagine, the dinner turned into a double celebration!

As I went down to the factory on Monday, my Voice tried to instill a little confidence in me. It was just like having a father with me all the time giving friendly advice. "Don't be scared," said my Voice, "if you are only there on trial, you haven't lost anything. It will all be experience for you. If you do as you are told, it will be quite all right. When you go there this morning and he tells you you've got the job and asks you if you are willing to accept it, you must say to him firmly that you will take the job but only on condition that he puts you in complete charge of the factory."

I bore in mind this advice, and when I arrived at the factory I told the owner that if he wanted his business pulled together, I would try and do it for him. But I said that I would only take the job if he left everything to me, because no business could have two bosses if it was going to succeed. Naturally, I would report progress to him and we would confer together from time to time, but I must have a free hand to run things in my own way.

To my relief, instead of showing me the door, as I half expected him to do, he said, "You're just the man I've been looking for. I want to be able to travel for three or four months at a time, and I want someone like you to be here to look after things for me."

"Right," I said. "That's good enough."

He then invited me to come with him and meet the staff, and showed me my office.

He introduced me to the girl who was to be my secretary, and generally tried to make me feel at home while he gave me all the information he could.

So I sat down at my desk and wondered what to do next. Then things started to happen with a vengeance! Customer after customer kept on ringing up to find out when their orders were going to be ready. Complaints of all kinds poured in from every direction, and I began to realize what I had let myself in for. Never have I suffered such a dreadful assault upon my nerves. I had not the faintest idea who the customers were or what their orders might have been, so I sought enlightenment from my secretary.

"Do you know anything about this business?" I asked.

"I've only been here three months," the poor girl answered. "I haven't a clue!"

Shocked to the core, I wracked my mind for a solution. Then I had a brain wave. Frenziedly seizing the telephone, I rang up the owner.

"Look, sir," I said, "this girl you've given me has only been here a short time, and she doesn't know one customer from another. The system won't work if I have to sit here all day answering customers' problems. So could you let me have your secretary to carry on here while I go around the factory and get things organized?"

"What a splendid idea!" he exclaimed, and I felt that my stock had risen a little, although I was really only trying to get myself out of a headache.

So down she came to my office, and I set off to see what I could see. My main objective was to familiarize myself with the type of goods that were being produced and to understand the processes of manufacture.

For several days I did nothing but walk around the factory and watch what was going on. All the time I kept my mouth shut and never uttered a word about anything, so that nobody had any idea that I was not an expert.

I learned rapidly from my observations and from watching small incidents that occurred. Sometimes when I walked into one of the workshops the foreman used to come around with me. To show how alert he was, he would occasionally pull up one of the men who was doing a job in the wrong way.

I showed myself to be duly impressed by his efficiency but refrained from comment. Then, perhaps a day or two afterward, I would be strolling through the same workshop and see a man committing precisely the same error. I would go up to the man and say sharply, "What do you think you are doing? That's not the right way to do it!"

The foreman would then rush up and say, "I've told him the same thing two or three times before."

"Oh!" I would reply. "Well, see that it doesn't happen again."

It was the foreman's turn to be impressed with my technical knowledge!

After a time things started to go more smoothly, and one day the owner came up to me and said, "I want you to go to Brussels for me."

"That's great," I thought to myself. It was not long since I had been there as a soldier, and I thought it would really be something to go back there as a civilian without the restriction of military discipline.

"What do you want me to do out there?" I asked.

"I want you to buy some glass," he answered, "and also find out about a certain process for decorating glass which we are not able to do in this country."

So off I went to Brussels, and, having completed my orders, I succeeded in making contact with some manufacturers who allowed me to look around their factories. I took note of everything to do with this special process of decorating glass until I had it all down pat, and then started for home again.

When I went to report to the owner, I said to him, "We're going into a new line of business!"

"What do you mean?" he said.

I then told him that I had acquired a complete knowledge of this new method of decorating glass and that I thought there was a fortune to be made out of it as the trade was crying out for the process.

He was delighted, so we bought some kilns and started up. We recruited a staff of girls, and with my newly acquired knowledge I was able to train them in a few days.

Very soon the new business "took off" in a big way and we had more orders than we could cope with.

Meanwhile, the original half of the business went on.

But, had I but known it, I was in for a shock. One Monday morning the owner said to me, "I'm going to give up the decorating part of the business at the end of the week."

I was dumbfounded. "Heavens," I thought, "this is really good, just as I had got things nicely settled."

So I asked him what was wrong, and he told me that he

felt things were getting a little too much for him and he wanted to get rid of responsibility on the decorating side and just keep the original part of the business for his son.

"What?" I said, feeling very upset. "Are you just going to close up like that?"

"No," he replied quietly, "I'm giving the business to you."

"Giving it to me?" I repeated in astonishment.

When I had recovered a little, it occurred to me that although this was a most generous gesture on his part it would mean my taking on a considerable financial responsibility. So I said that I would let him know at twelve o'clock that day if I could take it on.

I thought quickly and without more ado rushed to the telephone. I rang up several of our biggest customers and told them the owner was giving up at the end of the week. This threw them into confusion, and naturally they wanted to know what was going to happen to their orders.

"I'll tell you what I'll do," I said. "If you can send me some money on account, I will carry on the business." They agreed at once, and I went and told the owner that I would accept his offer, and thanked him.

The next morning all the checks arrived by the first post, and overnight I had become a big businessman!

The man who gave me this wonderful chance in my life was a German Jew who had left Germany on the eve of Hitler's rise to power. I shall never cease to be grateful to him for his great kindness and generosity.

The mills of God grind slowly, but they grind exceedingly small, and I was glad that I had obeyed my Voice.

2

Beginning of a Mission

For three years, things went extremely well, then suddenly I began to have the most peculiar experiences.

I do not drive a car, and it was my daily custom either to take a taxi or to walk to the bus stop and catch a bus to work.

Sometimes as I walked along the street I could not feel my feet upon the ground, nor could I feel my body. I could not make it out at all, and often I would sit down thinking that I was going to faint.

Occasionally I would be sitting in the bus and there, in front of me, I could clearly see lines of writing which I could read without difficulty. This was at once alarming and puzzling until I realized after a while that I was being sent messages in writing instead of hearing my Voice. Some of these happenings I related to my wife, who got very worried that I might be ill.

Then one night my wife and I had gone up to bed and I was sitting up making a few notes about business in the factory for the next day, as was my habit. Meanwhile, my wife had fallen asleep.

I looked up from my notes for a moment as I was considering a point, and—to my amazement—there before my eyes was a locket and chain which had belonged to my mother, just floating around the room. This further shock was just about as much as I could take and I thought to myself, "My God! What's happening? I must be going crazy!" In horror, I closed my eyes, then opened them again. It was still there.

Then it paused momentarily in its flight and clipped open in front of me, showing me the photographs of my father and mother inside it.

"This is unbelievable," I thought. "What's it all about?"

I knew that if I went to sleep there and then, I would certainly think that it had been a dream when I awoke the next morning. So, grabbing my pencil, I made a note on my pad: "Before I went to sleep, saw Mother's locket floating around the room."

This locket had been left me by my mother, who died while I was in the forces. I treasured it so much that I carried it everywhere with me in the breast pocket of my jacket, which was on this particular night hanging on a chair in the dining room.

I couldn't make out how a locket which was in my jacket downstairs could possibly be floating about my bedroom on its own. It just did not make sense to me.

In alarm, I quickly asked my Voice what it was all about. It seemed hours before it came through with the answer: "Don't worry! It's your mother. She has just heard that from tomorrow you are to be allowed to use the gift you were born with, because you are ready for it. She's so excited and wanted to be the first to tell you, but she didn't know how to let you know it was her. She hoped that you would understand that she was there by showing you this locket."

"But my mother has been dead for years," I said.

"You think your mother is dead," went on my Voice, "but this is not so. When people die they come over here to live with us, and your mother is here now."

Until I heard my Voice say this, it had never dawned on me that people lived after death—I do not know why—and it seems incredible that in spite of hearing my Voice all those years it had not occurred to me. Perhaps I was not meant to know until that moment—I do not know.

My next question, of course, was to ask what was this gift I was born with.

"Your gift," said my Voice, "is to heal the sick. You are born to be a healer."

"But I can't heal the sick," I protested.

"Yes you can," was the answer, "and we will prove it to you, but before this, we will give you confirmation through a person on earth."

I was also told that I must sell my business and devote all my time to healing.

The next morning I debated in my mind how I was going to break this news to my wife. I had never been allowed to tell her about my Voice, and now I had to tell her that I was going to be a healer.

I thought she would never believe me. Anyway, I had to do something about it, so I said to her apprehensively, "Grace, do you know what I saw last night before I went to sleep?"

"No," she said, as though she wondered what was coming now.

"I saw Mother's locket and chain floating around the bedroom."

"Don't be silly," she said. "You left it in your jacket pocket in the dining room. It was still there this morning."

Feeling very disturbed, I went off to my business.

On my way home that evening I was a bit nervous

because after our conversation in the morning, I thought I was going to get my leg pulled.

But to my surprise, when I got home I was greeted by my wife in a state of great excitement.

"Ted," she said, "you know the couple next door? Well, I was in the garden this morning and I saw the lady wanted to talk to me, so I went over to her and had a chat. I told her that you made me laugh this morning when you said you had seen your mother's locket floating around the bedroom. I expected her to be amused, but she wasn't. She was quite serious and said it meant that your mother wanted to get in touch with you. When I told her your mother had been dead for years, she said that made no difference because she was now alive in the spirit world. She said she knew this because she and her husband were Spiritualists. She asked me to tell you there is a famous medium coming to the town hall in three weeks' time and she thinks you ought to go down and see him."

As soon as she had said this, I knew that I must go and see this medium because this might be the confirmation that my Voice had promised me.

It was what I had been waiting for. The days would not go fast enough, and those three weeks before the meeting felt like three years.

At last the day came. The meeting was not until eight o'clock in the evening, but I was so keen not to be late that I left my office at four.

When it was time to go, I felt distinctly nervous, as I had never been to anything like this before. So I asked my wife if she would come with me.

"No!" she said. "I don't want to go to that sort of thing."

"Don't be silly," I said, "it'll be all right."

After some discussion I managed to persuade her, and she agreed to come with me.

We arrived outside the town hall and bought two newspapers to hide our faces behind in case anyone should recognize us as we were going in.

However, we safely got inside, and, being too shy to sit in front, we found two seats about halfway up the hall. We had never been inside it before, nor had we told anybody that we were going to the meeting.

The meeting started with a hymn, and then the medium, Joseph Benjamin, who was very well known, rose from his seat.

He began by giving someone a message, which meant nothing to me, so we sat back and waited.

Suddenly the medium took a step back on the platform and said, "I have the most wonderful woman with me here."

He then started to describe her in detail, and my wife whispered to me, "He's talking about your mother!"

"I know," I whispered back, "I can't believe it."

The medium's voice went on, "She has a most peculiar name. She is called Mrs. Fricker."

I felt myself go hot and cold all over.

The medium then said that she was telling him that her son had had a most remarkable experience a little while ago. This, of course, was the night when I saw the locket and chain floating around the bedroom.

"She wants me to find him in this hall and confirm that she had tried to get in touch with him."

He looked around the hall until his eyes finally fixed themselves on me.

"You are her son," he said.

I was speechless. When I had recovered a little, I said, "Yes, I am her son."

For an hour or more he recounted to me the whole course of my life from my childhood to that day.

He said that the reason I had come to the meeting was

the experience with the locket and that my mother had tried to get in touch with me to tell me that I was born with the gift of healing and would one day be a great healer.

The last thing the medium told me was that I would receive confirmation of my healing mission from one more person.

This whole experience was so wonderful that for some time afterward I did not know if I was living on earth or in heaven.

A few weeks passed, until one day I heard that a medium was going to hold a meeting in what was really a little tin church.

By this time I was quite prepared to go anywhere, and I was determined to attend the meeting.

It was to be held on a Sunday, and when the appointed day arrived I set off in great excitement for the little tin church.

There were about sixty people, and I gathered that they all attended regularly, and it seemed to me that I was the only stranger present.

The medium was a very old lady, Mrs. Turner, and her opening remarks gave me a keen sense of disappointment.

"Before I start this meeting," she began, "I must tell you all something because I don't want you to feel disappointed. I have been sent here tonight to give one message only. I have been told that after I have delivered this message I am not to do this anymore, that my work is done."

"Just my luck!" I thought. "It's sure to be for one of the regulars. A waste of time coming."

"I am honored," went on the medium, "to be allowed to give the message."

She paused, looked straight at me, and said, "You're

the one I want! God has blessed you, for you have been trained from childhood for your mission to heal the sick. One day you will become famous, and through this it will be recognized on earth that a great healing power exists for the benefit of all mankind. This is a part of your mission, which you will accomplish successfully before you pass over to the other world."

Here indeed was the confirmation which had been promised to me by Joseph Benjamin a few weeks earlier.

Finally she said to me, "Look at the words which God spoke to Joshua in the ninth verse of the first chapter of the Book of Joshua. God wants you always to remember these words."

When I reached home I opened the Bible and read: "Have I not commanded thee? Be strong and of a good courage, be not afraid, neither be thou dismayed: for the Lord thy God is with thee whithersoever thou goest."

(In order that I should not forget these words, I had them printed and mounted in a frame which I hung upon the wall of my consulting room where I can read them every day and can derive comfort from them when my spirit flags.)

I hesitated no longer. I was ready and willing to begin my mission.

How was I to go about it? There was first of all the practical matter of selling the business, which I had been told I must do. This would take time, and I was impatient to get started on my healing work. So I thought the best way was to compromise, and for the time being to carry on my business by day and take a few patients at home in the evening. But from where was I going to get them?

I told my brothers and my sister what I intended to do, and they thought it was something of a joke.

One day one of my brothers rang me up and said,

"Look, I've got a fellow you can try to heal. If you can cure him, then you *can* perform miracles!"

No doubt he was thinking that he would have a little fun at my expense.

Well, nobody so far had asked me to heal them, and I was so keen to have a patient that I asked my brother to send this chap down to the factory.

He duly arrived, and it turned out that for most of his life the poor fellow had suffered from a damaged spine, so that he was bent almost double, and he told me that he had treatment three times a week from an osteopath to ease the pain.

You can imagine my feelings! I had never tried to heal anyone before, and I had never been given any practical instructions at all. And this, my first real patient, looked in such terrible shape that I was too scared to touch him.

Anyway, it was too late to back out now, so I said I thought the factory was not a very suitable place, and that if he would come to my home in the evening, I would see what I could do for him.

I spent the rest of the day praying that he would change his mind and not come, because I did not see how I could possibly help him, let alone cure him.

Punctually at seven o'clock he turned up, and with much misgiving I led him into my lounge. I had not the faintest idea what to do or how to begin.

To cover my feelings I started to chat with him, and in a friendly gesture I put my hand on his back.

Without any warning I received the greatest shock of my life. While I was talking to him he started growing taller and taller until finally he stood up quite straight with a great shout, "I'm cured! I'm cured!"

I stood dumbfounded, unable to understand what had happened, until he said to me, "You frightened the life out of me. When you were talking to me I couldn't see you. I could only see Christ in His robes standing there!"

The very next day he met a friend of his whom he had not seen for ten or twelve years. The friend, who remembered what he had been like the last time they met, took one look at him and exclaimed, "How did you get like that!"

My former patient, who was still in a state of bewilderment at what had happened, replied, "I don't really know. My friend sent me to a chap who has got some healing powers. He didn't do anything much. Just put his hand on my back, and it straightened up. That was all."

"That's fantastic," said the friend. "I wonder if he could help my brother-in-law."

It appeared that the brother-in-law had been lying on his back in the hospital for a long time with paralysis of the spine, and he was coming home the next day on a stretcher before having an operation—not to cure him but to relieve the pain. So my patient telephoned me to ask if I could do anything about it.

By this time I was in such a state of excitement that I was prepared to try my hand at raising the dead!

"Right," I said, "bring him down to me. But how are you going to get him here?"

The chap thought for a moment and then came up with the idea that he would take the seats out of his car and get some friends to help him put in the stretcher.

And so they brought this poor man down to my house and laid the stretcher on the floor of my lounge.

I looked at him aghast. My mind was in a turmoil with all sorts of terrifying thoughts racing through it. I could practically see myself in prison because he had died on my hands.

To hide my confusion, I was talking to his friends about anything but healing, secretly hoping that they would take him away again, when he looked up from the stretcher at my feet and in a pathetic voice asked, "Can you help me, guv?"

I had been too scared even to address a word to him, but I heard myself saying, "Help you? I'll cure you in two minutes!"

And before I realized what I was doing, I found myself kneeling on the floor beside him and pushing my hand underneath his body. As soon as I touched his spine he jumped off the stretcher and stood up crying out, "I'm cured!"

I was left kneeling on the floor, not believing what was happening. The first thought that flashed through my mind was that there could not have been much wrong with him.

Meanwhile, the chap was going crazy with excitement. He told me all about his previous condition and the dreadful experience he had been through, which left no doubt in my mind that a cure had taken place which seemed indeed little short of miraculous.

The next morning he telephoned me.

"Mr. Fricker," he said, "I don't know what to do. The day after tomorrow the ambulance is coming to take me to the hospital for an operation."

So I told him that the only sensible thing to do was to go and see the surgeon and explain to him what had happened. When he asked if I minded him telling the surgeon about me, I said, "Of course not. Just tell him the truth."

So off he went to the hospital, and later he recounted to me what had occurred.

When he walked into the surgeon's room, there was a moment's stunned silence.

"My God! What's happened to you?" asked the surgeon at last.

"I don't quite know, sir," answered the man. "Some friends took me to a chap, and he just touched my spine, and suddenly everything was all right."

The surgeon gave him a thorough examination, working his arms and legs about until he had to admit that it appeared as though a complete cure had taken place. However, to satisfy himself, he took some X-ray photographs of the man's spine. After an hour the surgeon returned with the results, which showed that where there had been a damaged and distorted spine there was now a spine which looked as good as new.

"You're cured," said the surgeon. "I can't understand how it happened, but my advice to you is to go home and thank God for the rest of your life for guiding you to this man, whoever he is."

Two months later the man who had lain paralyzed on a stretcher at my feet won a high-diving championship, and six months after that, he won a competition in weight lifting.

Such remarkable happenings naturally could not go for long unnoticed, and very soon the newspapers got word of them.

One day I was telephoned by the local press and asked if they could come and see me. They had heard so much about these wonderful cures, and they wanted to see for themselves what it was all about. I said they could come down one evening and talk to me about it.

At the duly appointed time, four of them arrived, and I took them into my lounge, wondering what they were going to say.

"We've heard so many stories of extraordinary cures," they began, "that we want to put you to the test. We've brought a patient along with us, and if you can cure him, we'll give you a wonderful write-up. But if you can't, then we'll say it's just a load of rubbish."

By this time I had begun to have confidence in my healing gift, and I had no hesitation in agreeing. "Fair enough," I said.

They did not tell me which of them was the patient, nor did they mention a name. We all sat down, three of them on the sofa and one on a chair.

My Voice immediately came through. "Don't worry," I was told, "you must make this one of the fastest cures you have ever done. Do you see that young man sitting between the other two? He is the patient, and he is suffering from an ulcer. Count the third button up on his vest, and that is where the ulcer is. When we tell you, put your hand across and touch the place and tell him he's cured."

I looked straight at the young man and said, much to the surprise of all, that he was the patient and that he had an ulcer.

Without moving from my seat I reached out and put my hand on his third vest button, resting my other hand on his side.

"Right!" I said. "It's cured."

"Don't be ridiculous," they said.

"You made a bargain with me," I replied. "If you don't believe me, have him X-rayed."

"Oh, no," they said, "we know a much better way than that. All we have to do is to take him out to a restaurant, give him two whiskies followed by fried fish and chips, and if he isn't cured he'll be flat on the floor!"

Well, I heard nothing for a few days until the evening of the next publication of the weekly newspaper. Then the telephone rang all evening with people asking me if I had seen the newspaper and describing to me what it had to say about the astonishing cure I had performed on the patient they had brought to me.

So I thought that I must read this for myself, and I sent out for a copy. When it arrived there were banner headlines splashed all over the front page with an account of the "miracle" cure. They had certainly fulfilled their promise to write a good story about me.

It appeared that the patient was one of the directors of the newspaper, and after describing the instant cure I had performed without even getting out of his chair, the account went on to say how they had taken him straight from my house into the nearest pub, where they gave him six whiskies. Then they marched him off to a restaurant and gave him a huge steak with fried chips. He had been permanently on a strict diet and had not dared to touch a steak for years for fear of the painful consequences.

But this was only the beginning. The same treatment was meted out to him for six consecutive days, and the more whiskey they gave him, the fitter he got. It must have been a great party, and the picture it conjured up tickled my sense of humor.

The poor chap's ulcer had certainly been cured, but he must have had a most fearsome headache by the end of the week.

The newspapers have been of great service in bringing to many people's notice the existence of healing power, and through them many people have come to me for help who would otherwise never have known of me.

There was the case of a woman who was gradually losing her sight, and who had been told that nothing could be done to save it. Apparently this illness had attacked her mother and two of her mother's sisters, all three of whom eventually became blind.

One day she saw my name in a newspaper in connection with a cure which had taken place and decided as a last hope to come and see if there was anything I could do for her.

She came to my voluntary clinic in Tottenham and was surprised to find that there was a long queue of patients stretching into the street. At that time I was treating an enormous number of patients each week, laying my hands on many of them for only a few seconds.

When her turn finally came, I told her that I could heal her, but since her eyes were in a terrible state, it would take a very long time. I also told her that when she was unable to come to me I would give her absent healing if she would concentrate her thoughts on me.

After a time she felt a sensation in her eyes as though something was being done to them, but there was no pain. In spite of this, there was no improvement in her vision until one September she and her husband and two children decided to go to Blackpool for a holiday.

As they were walking along the seafront, she bent down to pick up something she had dropped. As she did so, she discovered that by putting her head to one side she could see a considerable distance. She could hardly believe it, but for the rest of the holiday she went about with her head turned to one side. Gradually her sight improved until she was able to see with her head in the normal position, and her eyes became completely healthy.

She was grateful to me for helping her, but she also thanked God for working through me to cure her.

It was only by chance that she had heard of me through the newspaper, but it is one of the ways by which people are guided to me for help.

After these fantastic experiences I realized that something had to be done about using my strange gift in an organized way.

There was now no shortage of patients, for the news of the cures had spread like wildfire and there was an endless succession of telephone calls.

I knew that it would be a long time until I could sell my business, so I started giving healing at home one evening a week from seven o'clock to midnight. As my cases increased, I extended treatments to two evenings each week, until the pressure became so great that I was doing it five evenings a week and all day on Saturday.

All this time I was working on an entirely voluntary basis, and I made no charge for treatment. I did this for two years. Then I was told by my Voice that the time had come when I must finish my business and give my full time to healing.

Well, I had not yet sold my business, so I thought I would take two whole days off a week to do healing, and hoped this would satisfy my Voice.

Anyway, I was doubtful if I would get any patients in the daytime. I need not have worried because patients arrived in unending succession.

While I was doing this daytime healing, I used to leave my manager in charge of things at the factory. One day the telephone rang in the afternoon. It was my manager.

"Come down at once," he shouted, "the whole place is burning down!"

"It serves me right," I thought to myself. "I should have done what I was told. Now I'm being punished for not selling the business."

Hurriedly apologizing to my patients, I jumped into a taxi and tore off to the factory.

My factory was built along the side of a large courtyard, and adjoining it was, of all things, a timber factory. When I arrived I was stopped at the gates because the timber factory was completely ablaze from end to end. For two hours I could do nothing but stand and watch helplessly, tortured by the thought of how stupid I had been not to do as I was told.

At last I was allowed to go inside to inspect the damage. The sight that met my eyes was horrifying. The timber factory was burned to the ground and was a mass of charred girders.

At the place where the timber factory adjoined my factory, there was a door in the wall. Unbelievingly, I looked at this door and saw a slight scorch mark in one corner. The fire had stopped exactly at that point, and my own factory had suffered no damage at all! Not even one piece of glass was broken.

The timber factory was owned by three brothers, and they were almost in tears. They were only partly insured, and the place was a complete loss. It meant they would never be able to start up in business again, and all the staff would lose their jobs. I was desperately sorry for them and wondered what I could do to help.

It so happened that these two factories were due to be pulled down in a year's time, and I was not only going to receive compensation, but I also had made plans for a new one that the local authority was going to build for me.

Then I had a brain wave.

"Look," I said, "I'll tell you what I'll do. I'm going to give my business up soon. Give me a month to get my staff new jobs, and I'll hand my factory over to you—and the new premises, too."

Finally the day came when I had found jobs for all the staff except one—the woman who used to make the tea.

So I telephoned to the brothers to tell them what had happened and said, "If you'll give this woman a job, I'll hand the factory over to you, and the whole thing will be yours."

They immediately agreed, and that was that.

It may sound crazy, but I was happy to do it. While I was standing watching the fire, I felt I had let God down by not doing what I knew I had to do and that I was being punished for it.

When I saw that the only damage from the fire to my factory was one slightly scorched door, I have never felt so relieved in my whole life—not because my premises were intact but because I felt this was a sign that I had not upset Him. The relief was so great that I would have given myself away!

Money has never meant very much to me. Even in my school days when we children never wanted for a shilling in our pockets because our father was earning good money, it used to give me far more satisfaction to hand sixpence to a pal who was short of cash than it did to spend it on myself. It gave me a wonderful feeling inside, which was worth far more to me than anything money could buy.

It is a sad reflection that our society is dedicated to the making of money. Children are brought up and go out into the world with the one idea of accumulating as much money as possible, without having been taught the value of the many other wonderful things in life which would bring them far more happiness. I have known men who have striven all their lives to make a fortune and in the process have so undermined their constitutions that they have to spend much of their fortune in trying to get rid of their ulcers. A certain amount of money is an unfortunate necessity, but beyond that, it becomes nothing but a burden.

I have always looked on my money as God's money, and I try to use it wisely, not only for the benefit of my family and myself but also to give a helping hand to those in need who cross my path.

So now at last I was free to devote myself to my real work of healing the sick. Instructions from my Voice, which up till then had been very scanty, poured in about the action I was to take. I was told of the doctors and healers from the other world who were going to advise me and work through me. There was Sir Herbert Barker, who had been a great expert on joints during his life on earth, and who is now even more developed in his knowledge of the subject; Dr. Muller, a German doctor who is a specialist in spinal disorders; and Abdal Latif, who deals with cancer, ulcers, and internal ailments. He wears an Arab headdress and once lived in Cairo. I can see these doctors and many others whose names I do not know. There are also thousands of helpers of all races—African, Chinese, Asian, European—many of whom I am also able to see from time to time.

I was told that I must be deeply sincere in the use of my gift. However, I must give only so many hours a day to my patients. At the end of that time I must live my own life as a family man.

A year after our marriage, my wife and I had moved into a flat at 40 Howard Road, Tottenham, but during the war my wife and our son, Derek, had been evacuated and we had given up the flat.

One day, when the "blitz" had passed over London for the last time, my wife met someone at her mother's house and happened to mention that she was looking for a flat.

The very next day who should call but the owner of 40 Howard Road, who offered to rent her the very same flat, into which we moved for the second time.

Some years after the war, when I had begun my healing mission, the second flat in the house became vacant. I badly needed this space for the increasing number of patients, but the owner did not want to rent it, he wished to sell the whole house.

So I bought 40 Howard Road and made the ground-floor flat into Fricker's Healing Center, as I called it.

I had promised that I would dedicate my life to this work, and that if I was to be a healer, I would try to be the best.

And so I gave myself up to the task I had been set.

3

We Live by Touch

People are sometimes surprised to learn that I have absolutely no medical knowledge at all. It is all the stranger because of the fact that when I was very young my one ambition was to become a doctor, but owing to economic circumstances it was impossible for me to have the necessary training. As things have turned out, it was all probably part of God's plan.

I have never read a medical book nor a book on healing in my life. My Voice has always told me not to do so, because if I had any medical knowledge of my own, it might conflict with what I am told to do, and so in order to avoid confusion, I just follow the instructions which are given to me.

When you come to think of it, medical knowledge is not really necessary because I have all the advice I need from the doctors in the other world. When I lay my hands on a person, I can see a picture of his internal organs and I am shown exactly where to put my hands on the affected part.

But for many people it is not enough for me to tell them that I just put my hands on them and it will cure them. Quite naturally, they want to know how this is possible, so I will try to explain how it happens.

When you are born, God provides you with a set of body tissues which are necessary for the proper functioning of the body and which store up power just like batteries. Batteries need recharging from time to time, and in a similar way your tissues require recharging, too. This is achieved through physical contact with other people, and by touching each other we recharge one another.

When you are in your mother's body, you draw enough power from her into your tissues to bring you into this life. When you are just born, if you were never touched by another human being, you would slowly die. But happily the doctor smacks you, the nurse washes you, and your mother cuddles you, and this has the effect of keeping you fully charged with power.

When you grow up, the same process takes place by shaking hands or being patted on the back.

The power comes directly from God, and because God is Spirit, He can make contact with you only through a physical body; hence the necessity for us to touch one another.

If the position should arise where a person becomes isolated for any length of time and physical contact is impossible with another human being, the problem can be overcome by concentrating his thoughts on someone he has known. Thus he can establish contact with the vibration of that person and draw power from him. Distance is quite irrelevant.

This power is also a healing power, and if you cut your hand, it is this power within your own tissues which causes the healing process to take place. Anybody can set a broken leg, but nobody has ever tried to find out what knits the bone together.

If you hurt your hand, you automatically rub it. Everyone does this, but nobody can tell you why. Even animals lick their wounds.

The instinct to do this is implanted in you from birth, and what the rubbing does is to gather the power from the surrounding tissues into the sore spot, which eases the pain.

I was told an interesting story the other day by a woman who brings me a little boy for treatment. He is the son of one of her friends, for whom she does this service.

Her own doctor told her of an incident which occurred when he was still at the beginning of his career.

It seems that many years ago he was acting as an assistant to a senior doctor who was attending a woman patient at the birth of her child. The unfortunate woman had been an unusually long time in labor and was in a very weakened state.

At last the doctor in charge was able to bring the baby into the world, but after a rapid examination he told his assistant to place the child on one side because it was dead. He turned his attention at once to the mother as he feared for her life.

The assistant put the baby aside as he had been told, and looking down at its perfectly formed body, he could not help thinking what a waste it had been for the mother to go through all this agony only to lose her child.

Suddenly he heard a Voice telling him to put both his hands on the baby. He hesitated and thought to himself, "I really can't do that."

The Voice spoke again, this time more urgently, and he obeyed without further delay. He placed his hands on the baby, one on the front and the other on the back of its body, and waited silently.

After a few minutes the child gave a thin cry. Startled

by the sound, the senior doctor turned to the assistant and asked, "What on earth did you do to bring the baby back to life?"

"I just put my hands on it," he replied in some bewilderment.

What the young assistant did not realize was that by putting his hands in this way on the baby, he was recharging its batteries with power from his body.

As I have said before, when a woman is carrying a child, she supplies it with power from her own body. In this case the mother had become weakened by a prolonged period of labor. When a person is sick, power is used up much more quickly, and so there was insufficient power to supply the child's needs because the mother's power was exhausted.

I also explained previously that if a baby is not touched by another human being, it will simply die.

The doctor who delivered this child touched it only for an instant and having decided it was dead put it aside so that he could attend to the mother quickly. He had not touched it for long enough to recharge it, and because it was God's intention that the baby should live, a spirit person told the assistant to place his hands upon the child, and in this way the child was recharged with power.

The assistant is now a full-fledged doctor, but he evidently never forgot this experience, and I am pleased to be able to record it as an excellent example of the necessity that we have to recharge one another by physical contact.

A great many people who have healing power and yet are totally unaware of the fact are used by God without their knowledge and their gift is not wasted.

We sometimes read in the newspapers of "miracles" which happen for no apparent reason. A blind person perhaps may be walking along the street and suddenly his sight is completely restored.

If we were in possession of all the circumstances of such a case, I feel sure that we should find that the blind person had possibly been guided across the road or helped in some way by a born healer, unaware of his gift, whose touch had recharged the blind person's batteries to the point where a complete cure had taken place. It was all part of God's plan that healer and patient should be brought together in this apparently random way so that God's power could be transmitted through one of the healers He has placed on earth for this purpose.

God has so arranged this transmission of His power that it operates only while we are actually on this earth. If we leave this planet, we can survive only as long as the power lasts in our bodies because we cannot be recharged outside the earth's atmosphere.

For this reason I believe that it is wrong for men to leave this planet and go into space for any length of time.

I feel sure that this is the reason why the three Russian astronauts did not survive. They spent too long a time away from the earth, and when the power in their bodies was used up, they passed on.

During the American Apollo 15 mission, the prolonged period of weightlessness apparently affected the heart rhythm of Colonel Scott and Lieutenant Colonel Irwin, and Major Worden suffered a loss of potassium in his bloodstream.

On previous missions, astronauts were found to have lost calcium from their bones.

The doctors were very concerned about the astronauts during flight, but when they arrived back on earth they were given a medical examination and their health was found to be satisfactory.

What the doctors did not realize was that they were being recharged as soon as they landed on earth by people shaking their hands and patting them on the backs and by the doctors touching them during examination.

I believe that if they had been out in space for a longer period, they might not have survived. I think that the only time we are meant to go to other planets where life is possible is after we have passed on from earth to our spirit life. After a time, if it pleases God, we may be reborn on another planet.

By trying to reach there now, I feel sure that we are interfering with God's great plan.

Not everyone is cured instantaneously. Some cases may take a few weeks or months or perhaps a year or so, but I keep on treating every patient who is sent to me until he is cured or his condition has been improved to the fullest possible extent so that the burden of his suffering is ligthened and he can once more resume a normal life.

This applies to about eighty-five percent of cases.

Of the remaining fifteen percent, there are a great number whose time to leave this world is not very far away. The day is already registered when their journey through this life will come to an end because the purpose for which they came has been fulfilled. In such cases neither I nor anyone else has the power to alter this.

Nevertheless, there is much that I can do to help them to understand what is to come so that when the spirit leaves their bodies they will have some idea of what to expect. This helps the spirit to rise more easily from the body and lessens the shock of their transition from this world to the other world. In this way they are comforted in the remaining days of their lives and the fact of the death of the body does not seem such a terrible thing after all.

I consider this to be a most important aspect of my

work. It takes courage both to live and to die, and people can do with all the help they can get to do either.

The mere fact that a patient is old when he comes to me is of no consequence if he has not yet reached the end of his span of life. Even if he is ninety years old, he may still live to be a hundred, and God has no wish that he should live out the rest of his time crippled or in pain.

Although we are sent into this world for a special purpose and the day we reach our goal and shall leave is already determined, this does not altogether rule out the measure of free will which God grants to us and to everyone else.

Our lives may be cut short by accident or perhaps by the action of others—whether innocently or otherwise—so that we may not have had time to finish our task.

In such cases the spirit is allowed to return to earth from the spirit world after a very short interval in order that the ordained span of life may be completed and the purpose fulfilled.

Once a patient comes to me, I keep him as long as it is necessary or as long as he wants to remain my patient.

Some who come for treatment have been given up by their doctors as hopeless cases, and as a last resort they decide to come to me in the hope of a cure. Some of them are impatient and expect a "miracle" cure after one or two visits, not realizing that instantaneous cures are not always possible and that some cases require months or even years of treatment.

Most of my patients come once a fortnight, and my helpers from the other world often give me instructions to tell to the patients to carry out during the interval before the next visit. It may be that they are asked to concentrate on me daily, or perhaps to rub vinegar or oil into their joints every evening.

Sometimes they return on the next visit and complain that they are no better, and when I ask them if they have carried out my instructions, they have to admit that they have not done so. God expects people to do something to help themselves, and if they will not bother to do so, why should He do anything to help them?

If they do not do what they are asked to do in between visits, then it will take much longer to cure them when they simply rely on a fortnightly visit for treatment.

I have said that it is not necessary for patients to have faith, but it is at least an essential that they should have hope and patience and be prepared to give the healing power a reasonable chance to work. Some do not and after a few visits decide that the whole thing is no good and go away to continue to live or die in unnecessary pain and illness.

There are some cases where the disease has progressed so far that although the patient's time to go may not yet have been reached, it is impossible to effect a complete cure.

I then explain the situation to them, and I can often do much to ease their pain and improve their general condition, not only physically but mentally, if they are in a depressed state of mind.

Everyone who comes to me receives help in some way, and they are given strength to bear their affliction.

Sometimes when I lay my hands upon a person, it is the first time on this earth that the power of God, flowing through me as the instrument, has touched them, and it brings a great feeling of happiness.

There is another type of patient who, although quite unconsciously, does not really want to get well. He has become so used to illness that it has become a way of life and without it he would be lost.

In some cases a patient has taken refuge in illness because it gives him a good reason for being able to avoid the responsibility and difficulty of living.

Sometimes life has treated a person so cruelly that he cannot face any further pain and the only solution is to escape into illness.

Even in cases such as these where I have effected a cure, it has only been a short time until they have relapsed once more into their former state.

Such people are greatly to be pitied, but the only one who can cure a patient of this kind is himself.

Some years ago I had a case of this type which is not without humor.

A man came to me for healing who had been persuaded by his wife to try it.

While I was treating him, one of my doctors in the other world said to me, "You will not achieve any result in this case for six weeks. The man has been granted sick leave on full pay for a certain period and he has still six weeks left. He is determined not to go back until the full time is up."

The patient, quite unaware of what I had been told, asked me if I could do anything for him.

"I could, if there was anything wrong with you," I said dryly. "But I can tell you this, you will be back at work in six weeks' time."

"That's exactly what I keep telling my wife," was his short but very revealing comment!

My advice to people in this state of mind is: "Snap out of it. Health is the greatest wealth, and you don't realize what you are missing!"

It is not only the patients themselves who are affected by their illness. Their families and all those around them are concerned for their welfare and sometimes suffer great anxiety, causing their own health to deteriorate. When the sick person is cured, the whole family is cured, too. This is something to be remembered, as well as the fact that God helps those who help themselves.

There are many doubters about the existence of the other world and of God's healing power. Perhaps this is natural until they have had some experience which makes them believe.

Once I had a patient who was herself a believer, but the friend who accompanied her was a complete skeptic. Indeed, she had done all she could to dissuade the patient from coming to see me. However, in the end the friend agreed to come with the woman to my clinic.

I was told by my helpers about the friend's lack of belief, and they told me that they were going to make her realize that it was true.

"You don't believe there is such a thing as another world from which divine healing comes, do you?" I asked.

"No, Mr. Fricker, I'm afraid I don't," she replied frankly.

Meanwhile, I was being shown a picture of a motor racing track with a race in progress. Suddenly one of the cars ran off the track and crashed in flames. As it turned over, I was able to see quite clearly the number seven inside a white circle on the car's side.

I was told to ask her if her son had been killed in a racing car.

"Who told you that?" she exclaimed in surprise.

I answered that I had been shown what happened by someone in the other world.

"If you still don't believe me," I said, "I will give you further proof. Was the number on the car a seven in a white circle?"

There was no need for me to say any more. She was

utterly convinced. To comfort her, I explained that her son was alive and happy in the other world.

I am sure that she was guided to me so that her eyes could be opened.

I love children, and it always gives me special satisfaction if I am able to help them.

One day a woman brought to me a little girl about ten years old who had had a withered arm and hand from birth.

I examined her, and it seemed to me that this was a case verging on the impossible, as the withered arm was considerably shorter than the normal one. Nor was I given any advice in the matter by my helpers and no indication of the possibility of a cure.

I expressed my opinion to her mother, whose response was a flood of tears. She said that she had been told by a doctor that it might become necessary to amputate the arm altogether.

I was so much moved by her grief that on my own initiative I promised to give the child healing in the hope of some benefit. So I treated her and asked the mother to bring her back to see me in a fortnight.

During that fortnight I treated a great number of patients, and when the mother returned I did not at first recognize her as she came into the room. Without any preamble she said, "It's all grown!"

"What has grown?" I said, bewildered.

Then the child ran into the room, and I realized who she was.

"You don't mean her arm has grown!" I exclaimed.

I looked at the child's arm, and it had grown to the same length as the other one, and the hand and fingers were almost perfect.

"When did this happen?" I asked.

"You know the day when we came to see you," she replied, "well, the very next morning when she woke up she came running to me saying, "Look, Mummy, it's grown!"

I have seen many startling cures in my time, but this amazed even me. Although I was given instructions by my helpers while I was treating the child, I was not told that she would be cured.

Perhaps it was meant to be a test of my own faith.

In my work of healing I am often faced with the most unexpected situations. Indeed, there is never a dull moment.

There was one occasion in 1968 when I received a telephone call from a man who announced himself as a Swiss doctor to a V.I.P. who was at that time staying in a London hotel. Without mentioning any names, he invited me to come to this hotel and treat the man whose personal doctor he was.

I said that I regretted that I was unable to do that as I had a waiting room full of patients.

"But you must come," he insisted, "this is a very important person indeed."

"I'm sorry," I replied, "all my patients are equally important to me, whether they be kings or beggars. However," I went on, "what I sometimes do when people have come from a long distance is to push them into the list when there is a cancellation. If you'd like to bring your patient down here, I will try to do this for you."

But he refused my suggestion, and I asked him to let me know if he changed his mind.

The next day he telephoned again.

"Mr. Fricker," he said, "I do most urgently request you to come and see my patient. We have come here especially to see you."

It occurred to me that he must have been given my name by someone, since I did not know who he was. Again I repeated my offer to fit in his patient if I could, and again he refused.

After two further telephone calls I was rung up by the owner of the hotel, who was a great personal friend of mine.

"Ted," he said earnestly, "I want to ask you a favor. Ex-King Saud of Saudi Arabia is staying in my hotel and has taken two complete floors of the building for his suite. He asked his Swiss doctor four times to telephone you, and he is extremely annoyed that you won't come, because he has come especially to see you. He is prepared to stay here as long as you want, but if you won't come, then he is going to pack up and go home. I will send a car for you or do anything you want, but please do me a favor and come to see him."

In view of the fact that he was a friend of mine who I knew had helped a lot of people, I promised that I would come to the hotel in my spare time so that it would not interfere with my other patients.

So I went to the hotel, where I was greeted by the king's Swiss doctor. I immediately asked how he had come to hear of me.

"Well," he explained, "we came to London to consult a surgeon about the king's osteoarthritis, from which he suffers very severely. I rang the surgeon, whose reply was that there was nothing he could do. 'There is only one man who can do anything to help,' he said, 'and that is Mr. Fricker, the healer.' "

The doctor had never heard of me, so he rang another surgeon, and to his surprise received exactly the same answer.

In desperation the doctor sent for a Swiss specialist and had him flown to London.

On the specialist's arrival the doctor asked if he could treat the king's osteoarthritis.

"Why did you trouble to send for me," asked the specialist, "when you have a man in London who can treat it? Mr. Fricker, of Wyndham Place."

"When the king was told this for the third time," said the doctor, "he was determined to see you, Mr. Fricker, and that is why I telephoned you."

I was then taken to a room where I was presented to King Saud, a magnificent figure of a man, but so crippled that he was confined to a wheelchair.

He was in a very bad way and I treated him once or twice a week for several weeks, and then one day I was told to tell him to get out of his chair and walk. Through his son-in-law, Abdal Rahman al Ghuneila, who was acting as interpreter, I said to him, "Now, sir, today you are going to get up and walk."

Rather shakily he rose to his feet and, towering over me, walked down the passage and back again.

I treated him for a little while longer, until the time came when he had to leave London. Before he went, he asked me what he owed me.

"Nothing," I said, "but, if you like, send a donation to the clinic; it will be used to help other patients."

He turned and said something to the interpreter.

"The king asks me to request you to wait for an hour," said the interpreter, "he has sent someone to the customs at London Airport to collect a gold watch which he has had specially made for you."

I told the interpreter to tell the king that I would have great pleasure in complying with his request.

After an hour or so, the most beautiful gold watch arrived, which the king presented to me. It was inscribed with the royal insignia and signed by himself. It was much too good to wear, and I preserve it as a memento.

It was disappointing that King Saud had to leave London before I had sufficient time to effect a complete cure.

He had arrived at the hotel in a wheelchair, but at least I had the satisfaction when he left of seeing him walk to his car unaided.

4

Health Is the Greatest Wealth

Everyone is surrounded by an aura, which is the only part of the spirit which is outside the body. To most people it is invisible, but there are certain people who have the ability to see it with the spiritual eyes.

Scientific research has been carried out on the subject of the aura, and its existence has been established beyond doubt.

As a healer, my aura is very powerful and of a golden color.

Not very long ago a patient asked me if she could take a photograph of me sitting at my desk. As she was about to take it, she discovered that she had forgotten her flashbulbs.

"I don't think there will be enough light without the flash," she said.

"Try it," I answered.

Soon afterward, she sent me the print, which was in color. Not only was it a perfect exposure, but clearly visible was part of the golden aura around my head.

It is through the power of this aura that healing is transmitted to the aura of the patient.

If a person is healthy, his aura is brightly colored, like

a rainbow, but if it is dull and gray-looking, then I know the patient is in a depressed or weakened state, and I set about recharging him with power from my own aura.

Every living thing has a spirit and an aura, including plants, trees, and flowers growing in the garden.

I love flowers, and they know I love them. Many people are kind enough to send me flowers, and my room at the clinic is never without them. Because the flowers know I love them, they give of their best for me, and they always keep fresh for a far longer time than normal.

There is an old-fashioned idea among gardeners that one should talk to plants so that they will grow better. I often walk around my garden and do this.

I can tell at once from a person's aura if he is possessed of healing powers even if he himself has no knowledge of this.

Many doctors are themselves healers, especially those with a strong sense of vocation. If only they would use their hands upon a patient instead of drugs, they would be surprised at the results.

I have told hundreds of people about the healing power which has been given them, and they are practicing successfully in various parts of the world.

Some years ago when I was still working in my clinic in Tottenham, a woman patient came to me who was very seriously ill. The medical diagnosis was a scar on the left lobe of the brain—probably congenital—and it was declared inoperable. The symptoms were distressing, for her legs would suddenly collapse and she had frequent blackouts.

When she first wrote to me I was fully booked, so I said that if she would concentrate her thoughts upon me I would give her absent healing. From the time of that first absent healing she immediately began to improve, and I continued absent healing for several months. With every month her health became better, until one day she came to see me.

I laid my hands on her, and my doctors told me that the scar on her brain had started to heal and that she could be cured in time. I told her this and she was comforted.

She visited me at regular intervals for eight months, and with each treatment she improved a little, until she was able to walk properly again, and finally she was completely cured.

Sometimes patients take time to appreciate that they really have recovered from an illness, and are apprehensive in case it should return. So in order to give them a feeling of security, I tell them that they can return for treatment at any time if they feel there is any recurrence of the trouble.

To my surprise she returned to me only a week later, and I asked her what was wrong. She replied that she was perfectly all right, but that she had brought me a message from her husband, who was a farmer in Somerset.

He was so overjoyed by his wife's recovery that he had sent her to tell me that if I would agree to go to Somerset he would build me a complete clinic where I could treat the people in that area, who had great need of help.

While I was thinking what a wonderful thing this man was prepared to do to help other people, I was told to tell his wife that there was no need for her husband to build a clinic for me, but that he must build it for himself, for he had been born with the gift of healing. I told her this and asked her to tell him that if he would get in touch with me I would explain to him how to go about it so that he could try it out. When he was satisfied that he was in fact a healer, then he could start to build the clinic for himself.

After she had returned and told him all this, he immediately telephoned me.

"Mr. Fricker," he said, "are you sure that this is so? It is true that I like to help people, but I had no idea that I had any such gift."

I assured him that it was the truth and said, "Try it out as I suggested, and before long, God will convince you that you are a healer."

I advised him to start healing patients in his own home until he was satisfied that the results justified the building of a clinic so that he could devote his life to healing the sick.

Gradually he realized that I had not been mistaken about his gift, and in time the clinic was built. He treated hundreds of people successfully for a number of years, until his work came to the notice of the church and he was finally invited by the bishop to practice healing in the churches—which he now does regularly, assisted by his wife.

Health is the most valuable possession which anybody can have.

The existence of viruses and bacteria on this planet which are inimical to humanity is common knowledge. Many people blame God for all the illness in the world today, but in fact much of the illness derives from our own foolish actions.

Unhealthy habits of daily life, dietary excesses, or the abuse of alcohol are only too common causes of sickness and have been so for generations.

But in this age a new hazard to health has been added—the dangerous pollution of the environment by the misuse of chemicals which find their way into our food supply. It is impossible to estimate the amount of foreign substances which enter the human body in this way, nor is it possible to know the number of vital substances of which the human body is deprived.

Each part of our body requires a special vital substance, whether it be the skin, the liver, or any other organ. If any part is deprived of its necessary nourishment, then it starts to degenerate, and, if unchecked, this can lead to all kinds of serious illness, including cancer.

The balance of nature is very delicate, and even a small disturbance causes a chain reaction which can be detrimental to our health.

No farmer can tolerate an excess of pests on his crops, but to exterminate them in such a way that all other harmless or even beneficial insects are also destroyed can have disastrous consequences.

If there are no bees, there will be no pollination of flowers and fruit blossoms, and if all the insects have been killed, there will be a dramatic reduction in the number of the very birds which help to bring the insect population under control.

Everything in nature has a purpose, which is to support the life of the world, and we ourselves are totally dependent for our survival upon the continuation of the natural sources of nourishment. Any interference with the environment affects the health of our bodies.

Life is an intricate process, and although science has brought to light much knowledge upon the subject, there is yet a great deal which is not fully understood.

When we see a caterpillar in our cabbage patch, how do we know that besides feeding itself the caterpillar is not injecting some substance into the plant which is necessary to our bodies? Even if we do not eat the cabbage, it will return to the soil and perhaps pass on the substance to future plants which are part of our food supply.

However, God has not left us altogether defenseless against the results of our own folly, and there are two ways in which the harm can be counteracted. One way is by the regular eating of pure honey, which I have been told contains all the essential substances which are necessary to our bodies.

If there are any bees or wild flowers left after the application of chemical sprays, then the bees must have collected whatever remains of these vital substances. I always advise my patients to eat this life-giving honey. It can even be helpful in the prevention and cure of cancer.

God has given mankind this wonderful natural food which contains not only vitamins but a dozen minerals which are essential for our bodily health.

In modern times this has been discovered by scientific analysis, but from the earliest days tradition has asserted the wonderful properties of honey.

There is frequent mention of honey in the Old Testament, and in ancient Egypt it was used both as a medicine and as a treatment for the healing of wounds.

It also has the distinctive quality of readily absorbing moisture from the air, which gives it considerable healing power because it destroys disease germs by depriving them of the water necessary for their existence.

The second way of overcoming the harm caused to our bodies by pollution is to drink plenty of water. This has the effect of flushing away any poisons which may have accumulated in the body. If we do not drink water, then these poisons remain in the body too long and do great damage. Also, when we eat our food a certain amount is absorbed, and if it is allowed to remain uneliminated for too great a length of time, microbes form in the body which have a bad effect upon the health. So at least one full glass of water should be drunk after each meal.

It is a good thing on waking to drink a glass of water, for during sleep the digestive processes have been at work and there is an accumulation of waste matter which requires flushing out before we start the new day. Tea and coffee are no use for this purpose. Only pure water will do, and it does not matter if it tastes of chlorine.

If people would observe these two simple rules daily, they would be much healthier, and a healthy body leads to a healthy mind.

In order to avoid some of the evil effects of pollution, I advise everyone who has a garden, no matter how small, to grow as many vegetables as possible for himself and his family, and in this way he can be sure that these plants are free of contamination by chemicals.

Farmers have to make a living like everyone else, but science has put in their hands the means of intensive production, which can be very dangerous.

The temptation to make more and more money is not confined to any one section of the community, but our greed has led to the pollution of rivers and lakes and the green pastures which feed our cattle, as well as the wholesale destruction of wildlife.

St. Paul says that the love of money is the root of all evil. This is something which we all know to be true but about which we are reluctant to take any positive action to mend our ways.

However, there are hopeful signs that the world is changing for the better. Many in the rising generation have quite different ideas from their parents, and often have I heard a father complain that his son will not follow in his footsteps.

But perhaps in their own way the sons are wiser than their fathers. They have seen the evil effects of the continual greed for wealth in the moral degeneration of the population, and they feel strongly that this is the wrong way to go about life. Their natural sense of values tells them that there are many other things which are more worthwhile than the greedy accumulation of money, which can lead to corruption of mind and body.

Of course money is necessary for our needs and our development, but once money becomes an object in itself it is apt to exclude all other thoughts from our minds, thereby hindering our spiritual progress, which is the purpose of our life in this world.

It is the love of money which is the evil, not the money itself.

If a man has ability, his success in making his business profitable is of great value to the community. It is what he does with the money that matters. If he uses the surplus money to help others in need, and does not merely spend it entirely in gratifying his own desire for pleasure, then it does not matter how many millions he makes.

There is plenty of scope for the relief of the grinding poverty and starvation in some countries today which is the result of the greed of other countries who have more than they require for their needs.

It is natural for a man to want a decent standard of living for himself and his family, but moderation is the keynote because it is not true that the more we have the happier we shall become. It is nearer the truth to say that the less we have after our needs are satisfied the more likely we are to find true happiness in the joy and beauty of the simple things of this world and the rewarding human relationships that God has freely provided for us.

I myself came from a working family where we had enough for our needs but not much more. But our lives were happy, and it was the simple little things of life which brought us the greatest joy. If I had to be born again, I would not choose to be born into a rich man's family.

The ancients used to hold that the greatest good that a man could have was a healthy mind in a healthy body, and we should do well to remember this.

Spinal trouble is almost as prevalent today as the common cold. Every other person one meets seems to have some trouble or other with his back. I am told that this is caused by the lack of essential substances in our food.

The majority of my cases over the years have been of spinal disorders and injuries, and, strangely enough, God has given me a particular aptitude in the healing of these complaints. Where instantaneous cures have taken place they have been in spinal cases or in cases of stomach ulcers, in which field God has also given me a special ability. I am grateful that I have been chosen to do this work.

Not very long ago a doctor's wife came to see me for the treatment of a duodenal ulcer from which she had suffered for twelve years. She had been told that it could not be cured except by means of a rather risky operation which she was unwilling to undergo. There was no doubt that she was very ill indeed.

Quite by chance she heard my name, and—in her own words, "without much hope and as a last resort"—she came to see me.

I examined her and discovered that the ulcer was of enormous size. I then began to give her healing treatment.

"It was an amazing experience," is her own description of what happened. "All he did was to place his hands lightly on my stomach and back. Suddenly a great force seemed to flow through his hands causing us both to shake like pneumatic drills. When he removed his hands," she goes on, "all the agonizing pain had disappeared. Placing his hands on my head, he made a rapid upward flicker of his fingers over my face and neck. A feeling of great peace and happiness replaced the morbid depression I had experienced for some months, about which I had not even told him."

It appeared that the smallest amounts of beef or lamb in her diet had caused her excruciating pain, and she could not believe it when I told her that she could go away and eat anything she liked. But she soon found out that what I had told her was indeed true, and she has been eating beef and lamb ever since then without any ill effects.

"Returning home that night," she said, "my family was delighted and flabbergasted to see me looking so well . . . and about thirty years younger."

In due course an X ray was taken which confirmed the fact that the ulcer was completely healed and the tissue was healthy with an absence of puckers or scars, which in itself was unusual.

The doctor's wife ends her description with these words: "That instant return to full health was fantastic, and words cannot express my gratitude and real joy after years of misery and pain. Thank God for Fricker and all who help him in his great work."

5

A Son of Nazareth

For fifteen years I worked in my clinic, and it was difficult to make enough from voluntary contributions to pay my staff and other expenses. I had to treat literally hundreds of patients a week to cover my costs. In the initial stages, cures took place with remarkable speed, perhaps in order that my clinic should become well known.

One day I was told that Sir Herbert Barker, who during his life in this world had been very well known for his work on joints, was going to be one of my advisers from the other world.

The first thing he said to me was, "You've got to start a clinic in the West End of London. You might stay where you are for the next twenty years and nobody will ever learn what you have been doing."

I saw the point of this because part of my mission is to make known to as many people as possible the fact that healing power really does exist.

I had learned from experience that I must do as I am told when instructions are given to me from the other world. So I set about finding somewhere to go, and asked several agents to look out for something suitable. I must have seen fifty different places, and I got tired of looking.

Then on a Wednesday an agent telephoned to say that he thought he had found just the right place for me, a house on Wyndham Place.

I was reluctant to go and see yet another unsuitable house, but because on a Wednesday I have the afternoon off, I thought I had better go and see it.

I had arranged to meet the agent there at one o'clock, and as soon as he put the key in the door, Sir Herbert Barker said to me, "This is the place."

Before the agent could open the door, I said to him, "This is what I want. How much is it?"

"But you haven't seen it yet," he murmured in surprise. "You are a funny chap!"

I had to look around inside, and it seemed quite all right except that it needed doing up a bit.

Now when I had originally discussed with Sir Herbert Barker his suggestion that I should move to the West End, he had told me that I need not worry about the expense of decorating and preparing the new clinic because this would all be taken care of by a woman who would come along and pay for everything.

The chances of such a thing happening seemed so remote to me at the time that I dismissed the matter from my mind.

The morning after I had told the agent that I would take the place for my clinic, a woman telephoned me.

She was in a very distressed state of mind and implored me to help her.

"What is the trouble?" I asked her.

"My husband is in the London Clinic," she said. "He has cancer, and they give him only two hours to live."

"Who gives him only two hours to live?" I asked.

"All the doctors," she replied, "including a leading specialist whom I had flown over from the United States."

I was considering what she had told me when suddenly Sir Herbert Barker came through to me. "Tell her that her husband won't die," he said.

"Your husband won't die," I repeated to her obediently.

"How can you say that?" she said. "I told you I've got the best surgeons in the world here, and they all say he'll be dead in two hours."

At this point, Sir Herbert Barker spoke again. "Tell her not to worry, and ask her to telephone you tomorrow."

So I relayed this message to her. "Don't worry," I said. "If your husband is not dead tomorrow, telephone me and we'll start from there."

The next morning she was trying to get hold of me for two hours from eight o'clock onward. She finally reached me at ten, which is the hour we always start work.

"Mr. Fricker!" she said in a state of great excitement. "How do you know these things? All the doctors here are amazed. My husband is not only alive, but he got out of bed this morning and had a wash and a shave, and now he's sitting up in bed having his breakfast as though there is nothing wrong with him."

Sir Herbert Barker came through to me again. "Tell her that her husband will be out of the nursing home next Wednesday, and ask her to bring him down to see you on Thursday."

I repeated this to her, and she seemed rather taken aback. "Oh, Mr. Fricker," she said doubtfully, "my husband is much better, but I couldn't really expect him to be out on Wednesday!"

I asked her to telephone me on Tuesday to let me know if her husband would be able to come out the next day.

The telephone rang on Tuesday afternoon. "How do

you do it, Mr. Fricker?" she exclaimed. "The surgeon has just told me that my husband has made such a remarkable recovery that he is well enough to come home tomorrow."

On Thursday she brought him to see me at my voluntary clinic, and she could not conceal her excitement and joy. In the course of conversation I asked where they lived. It appeared that their home was only a few hundred yards from Wyndham Place.

"I've just bought a new clinic there," I told her.

She thought for a moment. "Will you be going there on Saturday?" she asked.

I said that I probably would be going.

"Will you call in and have a drink with us if you have time?" she said.

I knew I would have plenty of time on a Saturday morning, so I accepted her invitation.

When I got to their home, I was made welcome by the whole family. They offered me a drink, and I said I would have a little brandy. When it was brought to me, it was more like half a pint!

They were all so happy about what had happened that it was a very cheerful party and I felt on top of the world.

After a while this woman said to me, "Mr. Fricker, will you do something for me?"

Thinking that possibly she wanted me to help another patient, I said, "Of course I will, if I can."

"Well," she said, "when the builders have finished their work, will you let me buy everything you need for this new clinic?"

"You can't do that!" I said, momentarily taken aback by her suggestion.

"Oh, yes, let her do it!" came a chorus from the family. "She's made up her mind."

Then I remembered what Sir Herbert Barker had said would happen.

I thanked her for her generous offer and left with a round of handshakes and expressions of gratitude from the whole family for restoring their father to them.

I wasted no time in getting things moving at Wyndham Place, and by the following Friday the builder had finished. That very day the woman telephoned and asked how things were getting on, and I was able to tell her that the builder was just finishing.

"Good," she said. "I'll send my car for you tomorrow morning. We'll go down to Whiteley's, and you can order anything you want."

The car duly arrived and we set off for Whiteley's, where she immediately got hold of the manager and told him that I was to be allowed to choose anything I liked and it was only to be of the best quality.

I have never spent so much money in about an hour and a half! She really got going, and I had hardly had time to make my choices before she had arranged for someone to come to Wyndham Place and measure for the curtains and carpets.

Within a fortnight the whole matter was completed, and what Sir Herbert Barker had told me would happen had, in fact, come to pass.

As soon as I could, I moved into my new healing clinic at 15 Wyndham Place to start a new phase of my mission. I named it Fricker's Healing Center, the same as my previous clinic.

The room where I work is like any doctor's consulting room. It has a desk where I can sit with my back to the window when people come to consult me about their various problems. In one corner is a couch where severely incapacitated patients can lie, and a record player which I very often use when healing. Music is a great healer, and it serves to produce a relaxed atmosphere, which makes my work easier.

In the center of the room is a piano stool, upon which my patients sit while I give them healing.

On one of the walls hangs a portrait in oils which was painted some years ago by a French artist whose wife was a patient of mine. At the top of the canvas there is some writing which was not put there by the artist. This is how it came about. . . .

After I had accepted the fact that my mission was to bring healing to the sick, there was one question which had constantly puzzled me for years: Why was it that God had chosen me and not someone else for this work? After all, I had never been a particularly religious person nor, as far as I could see, did I have any special qualification for such a mission. At last I decided to ask why this was.

Every night after I have gone to bed I am surrounded by spirit people who come to talk to me, not only the doctors who advise me but many others who help me to solve the various problems which my patients bring to me. Some of them help with the absent healing which I give to a great many people who cannot come to me. Perhaps someone might telephone me from New York or some other faraway place, and these helpers instantly explain to me the situation and tell me what answer to give.

One night I asked them this question: Why had God chosen me? They answered that sometime later on they would show me.

I have learned from experience that it is no good to go on asking the same question again and again because in that case they never tell you at all. So I waited patiently until about two months later when, as I was having my usual evening discussion with the spirit people, they quite suddenly told me that they were going to give me the answer to my question there and then.

I lay quietly in my bed wondering what was going to happen next. Before long I saw right in front of me in the bedroom a large screen, just as though I was watching a huge television set.

As I looked, I saw the unmistakable figure of Jesus walking along followed by a huge crowd of people. While this was going on before my eyes, I was being given a spoken explanation.

I continued to watch, and my attention was drawn to the small figure of a young boy aged twelve or thirteen who was trailing along about fifty yards in the wake of the crowd. He was wearing a long robe of many colors. He had sandals on his feet, and on his head was a little black skullcap.

The Voice said to me, "Do you see this boy?"

"The little boy in the long robe?" I asked.

"This was the kind of robe worn by the Jewish people in those days," went on the Voice, "and that boy was you! You so loved this man Jesus that you used to ask your mother to wake you early so that you could follow him all day long. This is the reason we chose you to come back and carry on His work of healing the sick."

Now I understood.

Whenever I speak of this to anyone, a memory comes back to me of the house in Jerusalem where I was born. I have never been there, and I do not know where this house is, but in my mind's eye I can see it clearly in a narrow street with its overhanging top story.

I then asked, "What was my name?"

"ASON," was the answer. "The four letters stand for *A* *S*on *O*f *N*azareth, the place where Jesus lived. So that you may not forget it, tomorrow we shall write it upon your portrait which hangs on the wall in your clinic in London."

The next morning I could hardly wait to get down to the clinic. Having arrived much earlier than usual, I went straight to my room.

There, written across the top of my portrait, was the name ASON, just as they had told me.

Now it has faded a little, but it is still there today.

On the wall opposite this portrait is a lovely picture of the head of Jesus in oils.

It was painted for me by a woman patient who came to be treated for cancer. She was cured and went on her way happily to lead a full life for some years.

I heard nothing of her during that time until one day she telephoned me and said that she very much wanted to paint a picture of Jesus for me. I said I would indeed like to have such a picture. This pleased her, for she told me that she was experiencing a most extraordinary compulsive urge to do this.

In due course she brought me the finished picture, which proved to be a most beautiful and sensitive representation of the face of Jesus. I know it to be a true likeness, for I have seen Him many times.

Sometimes I feel His presence while I am healing a patient, and when I look up, I can see Him standing beside me silently watching, as though He has come to make sure that His work of healing the sick is still being carried on.

How she came to achieve this likeness is a very curious story.

She told me that she spent some time going around churches and galleries to get an idea of the way in which she was going to depict His face. This activity proved to be quite unhelpful, because each picture that she saw had quite a different face. So she decided to see what she could do on her own.

One morning she collected a canvas and easel, some brushes and paints, and sat down on a stool to begin painting. That was the last thing that she remembered until she came to herself and saw the finished picture in front of her.

When she had gone home after leaving the picture with me, I asked my Voice about this strange happening. I was told that she was nearing the end of her time in this world and that they had been anxious for her to do this picture for me before she went.

Three weeks later she died of a heart attack.

I had a case of osteoarthritis which led to an interesting happening.

One day I was told that I must have a bronze head made which would serve, after I had passed over, as a permanent record of my work of healing the sick. I protested that I knew no sculptors, but I was told that someone would be sent to me in due course.

About a fortnight later a woman came for healing who was suffering from an arthritic elbow. She said to me, "I must get this elbow better because in my spare time I am a sculptress."

I wondered if this was the one they had promised to send to me. I was told to ask her if she could do eyes properly, and if she said that she could, then she was the right one.

So I said to her, "Can you do eyes?"

"Yes," she answered, "I can."

"Right," I said, "then you've got a job if you want it."

She was pleased that I had asked her to do the head in bronze and said that she would love to do it when she was cured.

Soon afterward, her elbow got quite better and she started on the sculpture. When the modeling was finished, she sent it to a firm to be cast in bronze.

While this was being done I received a telephone call from the manager of the firm, with which I was unacquainted. "Mr. Fricker, is this your head we're casting in bronze?" he asked.

"Perhaps it is," I said. "It's true that I have recently had a sculpture done."

"Well," he said, "the two men who were going to do the work took one look at the head and said, 'that's Mr. Fricker, the healer!'"

He said that he had cast hundreds of sculptures and never had he known one to be recognized on sight like that.

The head was duly delivered to me, and it truly was a marvelous likeness. It was beautifully executed, particularly the eyes. I suggested to the sculptress, because I thought it would help her, that she should send it up to the Royal Academy. She did so, and it was accepted and placed in the 1974 exhibition. I am happy to say that it brought her artistic recognition and today she is famous.

The bronze head now stands upon a marble pedestal in my consulting room at Wyndham Place.

I also have a little statuette in wax, which is not in my room, but which I keep at home in a glass case.

A woman came to see me one day who was suffering from a complaint which happily turned out to be of a not too serious nature. I treated her, and she came to me a second time, which was not really necessary because she was cured.

She was a delightful person, and we passed most of the second visit in pleasant conversation during the course of which I asked her what her occupation was.

"Have you ever been to Madame Tussaud's?" she said.

"Of course," I replied.

"Well, I make wax models there," she went on. There was a short pause. "Would you like me to make one of you?" she asked.

I protested that I did not want to her to go to such trouble. But she insisted, and I said that I would like her to make a miniature model of me. She said that, as she would be doing it in her spare time, it would take about four years.

Time passed and I forgot about it, until one day about four years later she rang me up to say that the model was finished. I thanked her and asked her to bring it around.

I was a bit doubtful as to how she could have made a model that was anything like me as she had only seen me twice for a few minutes. However, I thought to myself, "I must try to look pleased, even if it's awful!" I had no wish to offend her after all the trouble she had taken to do it for me. When she arrived, there was I, doing my best to look pleased!

She took off the lid of the box and started to unpack it. As she lifted the model from its wrappings, I could not believe my eyes. The likeness was startling.

There was the figure of a man sitting in a relaxed attitude with his spectacles in his hand, for all the world as if he had just taken them off. I was depicted standing behind him giving him healing, and she had dressed my figure in the exact clothes which I had been wearing when she last saw me. Every detail was correct, even to the little yellow dots on the tie, and an exact replica of my watch encircled the wrist.

I did not try to look pleased anymore; I *was* pleased as well as amazed at her wonderful skill, and my thanks were genuine.

6

Friends on Harley Street

When I decided to set up my healing center in the West End of London only a short distance from Harley Street, I realized that I was facing a challenge.

I knew that sooner or later the doctors would hear of me and, under the scrutiny of so many eminent members of the medical profession, I felt that I had to demonstrate beyond doubt that my healing power did in fact produce results, however unorthodox it might seem. Many dedicated doctors are themselves healers but do not realize the fact.

I had been at Wyndham Place about six months when I had a telephone call from a surgeon who to my surprise said that he wanted to thank me for all the help I had given him. I said that I was totally unaware of having done anything for him. He then told me the reason for his call.

He said that his wife, who had for a long time suffered from a serious spinal disability, had come one afternoon into his consulting room. He was astonished to observe that the disability had apparently vanished. He asked her what on earth had happened, and she replied, "You know that Mr. Fricker our friends told us about? Well, I went to him this morning."

"How long were you there?" was his next question.

"About three or four minutes," she said, with a smile.

"Unbelievable!" he exclaimed.

He went on to tell me that he had tried to explain it away to himself as a happy coincidence, but somehow this solution did not quite satisfy him.

Then an idea struck him.

His daughter also suffered from a similar spinal complaint, and he decided that the best way to settle the matter in his own mind would be to send her to me. If I cured her as well, then he would have to acknowledge that his wife's recovery was not just a coincidence.

So an appointment was made, and once again an immediate cure followed.

In all, he sent me eight patients who were instantaneously cured. After the seventh patient had been successfully treated, the surgeon called a conference with some of his colleagues, and they decided to send me an apparently hopeless case of paralysis from spinal injury.

They chose this particular patient carefully, not only because they considered him incurable but because he himself was a doctor. This, of course, I did not know at the time. He was asked to report to the other doctors after the treatment, and to give a full account and his professional opinion about everything that occurred during the healing.

When the patient arrived, he had to be helped into my room. He asked me, "Do you think you can help me, Mr. Fricker?"

"I'm going to cure you in five minutes," I told him, "and you'll be running around this room."

"Oh! I don't expect that," he said doubtfully.

"Well, I've promised," I said. "Now I've got to do it."

I asked his two friends to support him while I treated him, as he could not sit up on his own.

After a few minutes my Voice told me to tell him to get up. I did so, and his friends made as though to help him.

"No," I said, "let him do it himself."

After some hesitation he rose to his feet, whereupon I told him to walk. Very gingerly he started to put one foot in front of the other, until with growing confidence he drew himself up and walked around the room.

I do not know who was the more astonished, himself or his friends.

Thanking me, he returned immediately to the surgeon who had sent him, and half an hour later I received the telephone call.

The surgeon added that he had been careful not to let me know that he was sending me patients, so that I could not give them any special treatment. But he was very puzzled by the whole thing.

I said to him, "What you do not realize is that it is not I who cured these patients. The One who works through me must have known that you were sending me patients as a test, and so they were instantaneously cured as a living example of what healing power can do."

Since the day when the doctor was able to walk and once more resume his normal life, he has sent to me at least five hundred patients suffering from a variety of diseases including cancer, leukemia, and spinal disorders, the majority of whom have been cured. To this day he is still sending me patients.

As time went on, I made many friends in the medical profession.

One day a surgeon came to me as a patient. For about twenty-five years he had suffered from a gastric ulcer, which had made it necessary for him to take the greatest care of himself in order to relieve the distressing symptoms. But at last it had become so much worse that he was unable to do his work properly because of his inability to bend his body forward without a great deal of pain.

It was suggested to him by a friend that he should visit me and ask if there was anything I could do. An appointment was made, and when he arrived he told me all about it, although in fact as soon as he came I was told by my doctors in the other world what the trouble was. However, I like patients to tell me their symptoms because it relaxes them and is a perfectly normal thing to do.

I was told to tell him that I would be able to effect a cure very quickly, but I could see by his expression that he was slighty skeptical about this.

He removed his jacket, and I approached in order to lay my hands on him. He recoiled in alarm, saying, "Please don't touch me. The ulcer is so sensitive."

So I reassured him that my touch would not hurt him in any way, and he allowed me to place my hands on him. Immediately I could see the ulcer, and my doctors told me exactly how long to hold my hands there. Suddenly I saw the whole ulcer dissolve and disappear. Removing my hands I said to him, "It's all right now. Hit yourself in the stomach!"

He refused, saying that he dared not do such a thing. So I raised my hand and gave him a gentle blow on the exact spot where the ulcer had been. His face registered astonishment as he gently felt his stomach, until the realization came to him that he felt no pain at all.

I asked him to return in two days' time so that I could check that no vestige of the ulcer remained.

When he came back to see me, I asked him how things were going, and he answered me in these words: "Mr. Fricker, until I came here, I thought I was one of England's greatest surgeons, but after what you did for me two days ago, I realize how very little I know about these things."

A patient came to me eighteen years ago; he was one of Winston Churchill's cousins. I had previously cured him of tuberculosis, but on this occasion he was suffering from a growth on the throat which the doctors advised him to have removed by surgery if it was not to prove fatal. However, he had sufficient faith to come to me to see if I could do anything.

I treated him a few times, and each time the growth seemed to be getting larger, until I became very anxious. But my anxiety was allayed when one day the doctor in the other world who was advising me told me to tell the patient not to worry but that at two o'clock the next morning the growth would finally burst and he would be well again.

The patient left me and went home, and, as he had been told, the swelling burst at two o'clock in the morning. He got up in excitement and roused the household. He showed them his throat where the huge growth had been. There was not a mark to be seen. It was completely healed.

There is a sequel to this story.

Quite a long time afterward, Winston Churchill's cousin was sitting at dinner in his club when he was joined by a friend who was a well-known lawyer. He appeared to be extremely depressed and said he was suffering from a cancer of the nose, and that he was going to undergo surgery which might mean the removal of an eye and part of his nose.

Winston Churchill's cousin said to him, "Don't let them do that. Why don't you go and see my friend, Mr.

Fricker? Tell him I sent you, and ask for an appointment."

This the lawyer did, and I arranged for him to come the next day as there had been a cancellation. When he arrived I treated him, and I was told that he could be helped. So I asked him to come back and see me again.

"I can't," he said, "I'm being operated on tomorrow."

"Look," I replied, "you can have your eye and nose removed anytime. A few days are not going to make any difference."

So I finally persuaded him to postpone the operation for two weeks.

I treated him once more five days later, and I was told that it was getting better, although outwardly there was no change. Three days later he came again, and as he walked into my room, I looked at his face and there was no trace of the cancer to be seen. He could scarcely believe it and hurried away to see his surgeon, promising to return and let me know the result.

The surgeon, who was a leading cancer specialist, confessed himself to be astonished, for he could find no sign of the cancer, and asked the lawyer what had happened. But he would say nothing until the surgeon, assisted by two other doctors, had examined him and pronounced that he was completely free of cancer.

Then the lawyer recounted the story of his meeting at the club with Winston Churchill's cousin, who had suggested that he go to a healer. One of the doctors interrupted him to ask if the healer's name was Fricker, whose clinic was on Wyndham Place. When the lawyer replied that this was in fact so, the doctor said, "He is the only one that I know who could have done this."

The surgeon had no further advice to give except to tell him to thank God that he had been sent to a healer with the power to accomplish such a cure.

Recently I had a case which turned out to be one of those associated with Christmas, but this time Christmas brought some very unhappy experiences to the patient himself on two successive occasions.

David Adkin was a thirty-five-year-old bank manager with a family. Just before Christmas 1974 he visited a hospital for two days of exhaustive eye tests, which—in the opinion of the specialist—showed that his eyes were in an advanced and irreversible state of disease. "You could be blind within three weeks," was his bluntly but kindly delivered verdict.

"The glass of martini given me by the doctor to celebrate Christmas did nothing to melt the numbness of mind at that time," says David Adkin. "This news was the worst possible Christmas present."

Five of the six eye specialists who had studied his case declared that in their opinion his situation was hopeless and long past the point at which recovery could be made.

Because the local infirmary had not the facilities to perform the necessary treatment, it was arranged that he should be admitted to one of the leading eye hospitals in the forlorn hope that some amelioration might be made.

But it was all to no avail, and in spite of treatment at regular intervals, there was not sufficient improvement to enable him to resume work, which seemed the immediate goal. "As time went by, the hopes I held of going back to work were getting as dim as my eyesight," is David Adkin's way of putting it.

Gradually he was having to give up the social and committee work in which he was interested, but he decided to keep on attending the committee meetings of the Didcot Town Football Club.

"It was at one of these meetings, in March 1975, that the president of the club, a local coal merchant, set me on the road I had been seeking," says David Adkin. "He asked me how it was progressing, and I had to give my stock answer: I wasn't really improving. He said that he had a friend and customer who, as well as ordering a ton of nutty slack, had given him the name of some faith healer who had done wonders for people. The president urged me to see this man, Ted Fricker, who had a healing center in London, as he felt that it might do some good."

This seemed to David Adkin the soundest piece of advice he had so far received.

Nevertheless, he was filled with doubts, but eventually he decided to write because he felt that if he indeed went blind he would always regret turning down the chance of a possible cure.

"I was able to find my own way to the healing center," goes on David Adkin, "but was uncertain what I was going to find there–feelings shared by most people, I learned later. It was a very relaxed atmosphere with soft background music, which is so soothing.

"My second visit to Mr. Fricker was very significant. I remember it for two reasons. I am not superstitious, but it was Friday, June thirteenth. It was just two days before I was to go into the hospital again for further treatment to my eyes.

"Mr. Fricker assured me that I would not go blind, and this was the first positive news I had received from anybody about a recovery. This encouragement, coupled with a strange 'inner feeling' of something unusual happening, spurred me on my way with renewed hope to face the treatment.

"On Monday, June 16, my birthday, I was given extensive treatment to my left eye, and the following day I was summoned to appear before the specialist, as was customary, for the appraisal to take place.

"I was quick to realize that something quite extraordinary had happened to the eye. Seven doctors were brought to look at it. Words like 'remarkable,' 'fantastic,' and 'quite incredible' were used. They were unable to explain what had taken place or how it had happened. Mr. Fricker's assurances were confirmed.

"This success achieved on my left eye now demanded that all efforts should be put into getting the right eye rid of the fog which was clouding the vision.

"I had never expected Mr. Fricker to provide an instant cure. My faith in God and Ted as His human agent through whom the divine healing power flows was most important to me and it never diminished at all.

"My right eye continued to cause concern and at times seemed to be beyond recovery, and again doctors told me that I must accept that fact. I was getting confident, for had I not heard all that before and had not Mr. Fricker won through for me? Nor did Mr. Fricker ever lose his confidence that all would be well."

It was eventually decided by the specialist that an operation would be necessary on the right eye to remove the vitreum by surgery.

Whilst waiting over Christmas for a second time to be called to the hospital, the patient was told that this was an extremely delicate operation with no assurance of success.

The day of admission to the hospital for the operation arrived, and David Adkin's mind was in an agony of uncertainty about the wisdom of taking such an appalling risk. In desperation he came to Wyndham Place to see me on January 16, 1976, and I explained to him that my helpers would be with him while he was in the hospital, but that I did not think that the doctors would go ahead with the operation. This possibility seemed remote to him at that moment, as the doctors were determined to do it.

He left Wyndham Place and went to the hospital, where he spent sixty hours in bed with both eyes bandaged. He was then prepared for the operating theater, and the doctor came to see him before he was finally taken there.

The doctor removed the bandages and carried out an examination of the right eye. David Adkin suddenly noticed a look of surprise on the doctor's face. After a further examination the doctor told him that the condition of his right eye was so immensely improved that an operation was now unnecessary. Without further delay he was sent home and immediately returned to work.

"Mr. Fricker's predictions had come true," he goes on to say. "I still have my eyes and sight. I have not gone blind, and I never cease to thank God for the work of Ted Fricker. He has been an inspiration to me.

"In my experience I do now believe that orthodox medical science and faith healing, God-inspired, can go hand in hand to complement each other. I believe that my case proves this fact beyond doubt."

What more can I add to David Adkin's story except to say that I entirely agree with his conclusion?

There is an increasing number of doctors, however, who are beginning to realize the value of healing power when the limits of medical resources have been reached.

I had a woman patient sent to me by a doctor who had done all that was possible for her without success. Having heard of my work and being greatly concerned for the welfare of his patient, he advised her to come to me in the hope that, as the last resort, healing power would provide an answer to her problems, which seemed insoluble.

She had suffered very severe injuries in a car accident and for two years had been almost unable to walk. She was in continuous pain and was subject to "blackouts" which were caused by the injuries to her head.

During this period she had been under constant care in hospitals and nursing homes where she had undergone several operations including plastic surgery—all to no avail.

One day her doctor suggested that she should come to me for healing treatment, but she was very skeptical. At last she reluctantly agreed to try and see what I could do for her, and the doctor made an appointment for her to come and see me. Her condition was so bad that she had to be accompanied by a nurse.

From that moment she began to improve, and this was a continuous process until finally she was able to walk again and no longer suffered from "blackouts."

She took up her ordinary life once more and now runs two businesses herself because of the doctor who was prepared to admit that the limit of medical help had been reached and placed his concern for his patient as a human being before all else.

Some of those who may read this book will perhaps have difficulty in accepting the truth of the existence of healing power, which would not surprise me, because they have not had the experience themselves.

Many doctors do accept it, however, because they have seen the results in patients whom they have sent to me as being incurable. Some doctors have come to me as patients themselves and know the truth of it from personal experience.

I do not suggest for one moment that the medical profession should be entirely superseded by healers. What I would like to see would be a system of medical treatment in which doctors and healers could cooperate.

When a person becomes ill, he should first of all consult his doctor in the usual way. If after a reasonable time the illness persists and there is no further treatment which the doctor can offer, then is the time to visit the healer. The doctor and healer can both treat the patient at the same time, and this cooperation will serve the best interests of the patient.

Perhaps it could be arranged that a healing section could be attached to every hospital, consisting only of a healer and a nurse to help with the patients. When the doctors had done all they could for a patient, he could then be passed on to the healer in the last resort.

There are a great number of healers in the world, many of whom are gifted specialists in particular types of disease.

There are many more who do not know that they are healers but who would begin to come forward once the subject of healing became more widely known. I am able to tell at once if a person is a true healer, and there would have to be a selection of healers according to their gifts by someone like myself who has the ability to do this.

It is a dreadful thing to consider the possibility of a young person of perhaps twenty years of age having to live out fifty more years of life in a crippled condition. He has to be told sadly that he has to "learn to live with it."

The medical profession is dedicated to the relief of human suffering, and they do wonderful work. But medical knowledge has limits and, unhappily, such tragedies occur frequently.

Would it not be preferable if the doctors were able to tell the patient that the time had come for him to be treated by the healer, who might be able to help or even cure him? At least the patient would be given one more hope, and he would have nothing to lose and all to gain.

But even better would be if the doctors would call for the services of the healer before this stage had been reached. Most of the patients who come to me are those whom the doctors have given up as hopeless. If they were to come to the healer in the initial stages of the illness, a great deal of suffering and time and trouble would be saved, not to mention the expense of drugs and treatment.

The proof of the existence of healing power must come only from the results obtained.

There are many doctors who have sent me patients, and some who have been my patients themselves and are convinced of the existence of this power. But there are many more who are not satisfied and do not accept this free gift of God to mankind because it appears unorthodox and alien to established medical practice. I can very well understand their point of view, because this conservatism of outlook is a safeguard against quacks and charlatans.

I am quite prepared to appear privately before a board of doctors and demonstrate the truth of healing power if they should feel inclined to invite me to give them practical proof. If I were allowed to work in a hospital for a few weeks, this would do much to dispel any doubts they might have.

As I have said, it is God's power which works through me. I am only an instrument. I am not interested in proving that I am right and they are wrong not to recognize this power. All I want to do is to put at their disposal a force which will be of inestimable value in the relief of pain and suffering and which will contribute to the greater health and happiness of all God's children.

It is my sincere wish to achieve this cooperation with the medical profession before my time comes to pass over.

7

Return to the Other World

As I have already said, when you are born, the day is registered when you have to return to the other world. Each one of us is sent here for a special purpose, although we may not know what it is. Even a newborn child who lives only for an hour has in some way fulfilled the objective for which he was sent. Perhaps his death may serve to bring the parents together in mutual sorrow, or some medical knowledge may be learned which could be of service to others in the future.

During my twenty-five years of healing I must have treated close to a million people. Whichever walk of life they come from, they all have the same virtues and vices, the same strengths and weaknesses, and I love them because they are God's children.

Most of them are apprehensive about what is likely to happen to them when they pass to the other world, and they often question me about it.

For instance, I have been asked over and over again: "Mr. Fricker, I have had two husbands in my life. Which one will be my husband when I pass over?"

At first sight it seems a difficult problem, but, in fact, the answer is quite simple.

Marriage is an earthly relationship instituted for the orderly arrangement of society in order to ensure the bringing up of children to maturity in secure surroundings, and to that end it is protected by laws. But when we pass on to the spirit world, we leave behind our physical body and are no longer subject to those physical urges and attachments by which nature ensures the procreation of children.

The relationship in the spirit world between male and female is that of brother and sister. Indeed, there is love in the spirit world, but it is not the love of physical desire. As Jesus said when the question was put to Him, there is no marriage in the next life, but we shall all be "as are the angels of God in heaven."

It does not matter how many husbands a woman has had, for she will love them all without any jealousy arising.

Nor is it necessary to be afraid of meeting someone in the other world whom you have wronged on earth or who was your enemy. You will not be punished for what you have done to him, nor will he seek to wreak vengeance upon you.

We leave behind not only our physical body but all those animal feelings and emotions which are associated with it and which were designed by nature for the protection of the body's survival.

The essence of the spirit emerges from the physical body as a butterfly from its chrysalis and finds itself able to live in perfect harmony with all others in the spirit world.

The spirit world, which is situated outside the physical universe, is divided into seven separate planes of existence. We are sent to live in that plane which is particularly suited to the level of evolution which our spirit has reached. Those in the higher spheres can visit their friends upon a lower level, but those on a lower plane are not permitted to visit the higher until such time as their spirit has evolved sufficiently.

We are placed upon this earth to lead a physical existence in order that we may learn from our experience certain lessons which will help our spiritual evolution. If we fail to learn a lesson, we may be sent back to this earth in another physical body. The period of our stay in the spirit world may vary from a short time up to perhaps a thousand years.

This rebirth may recur more than once.

On the other hand, if our spirit has become very advanced in its evolution, we may be sent to another physical life on a different planet on the other side of the universe. There we shall be able to achieve a higher state of evolution by living on a planet inhabited by much more highly developed beings.

When a genius is born on this earth, it is because his spirit has lived upon one of these more advanced planets, and he is born into this world with all his acquired knowledge and skill. Such are the great composers, artists, and scientists whose genius shows itself from early childhood.

The reason for their rebirth upon this earth is that they may not have succeeded in their new life upon a higher planet and have therefore returned to earth to fill in the gaps in their experience by learning some previously uncompleted lesson. From the higher planet they have returned "home" to the spirit world and after a period have then been sent once more into this world to acquire the development necessary for their spiritual advancement.

This world is a testing ground, and during our life we

shall encounter both good and evil. But God has given each one of us a spirit person to guide us down the right path. We also are free to make our own choice, and if we choose a path contrary to the advice of our spirit guide, then it is our responsibility alone.

If we let our minds reach out toward God, then we shall receive this guidance in the form of a thought put into our minds, and it is then up to us either to accept it or reject it.

It is sometimes hard to understand why there is so much suffering in the world. But it is really all part of God's great plan for the evolution of the spirit in all of us. It seems that we are only able to learn through suffering, for until pain touches us personally, we cannot truly care for the suffering of others.

Nothing happens in this world without a purpose. I have already mentioned the fact that up to the age of twenty-one there was hardly a day when I was not suffering from one illness or another. Had it not been so, I should not have been able to understand and sympathize with the plight of my patients some twenty years later. It was all part of the preparation I had to undergo for my mission of healing.

The following story may perhaps help to illustrate the way in which God teaches us the lessons we have to learn, which is the purpose for which we have come to this earth.

Jim Johnston was a married man with a thirteen-year-old son, David, whom he describes in his own words as "not so much the apple of his father's eye, but a complete orchard."

Jim had worked hard and had been able to retire early with a satisfactory financial settlement. He was looking forward to many happy years at home with his family. But it was not to be. Only a few days of his retirement had passed when David suddenly developed a swelling in his throat.

He was examined by an Indian doctor who suggested that it would be helpful to have a second opinion, which surprised David's father, who did not consider it to be a very serious matter.

But the two doctors decided that David must go at once to a hospital, from which he was almost immediately transferred to yet another hospital in London. There he was placed under the care of a leading specialist who regretfully informed Jim Johnston that David was suffering from acute leukemia. The prognosis was not good. He was told that if his son responded to treatment, he had a maximum of ten months to live.

Jim Johnston's world was shattered.

"Why David," he asked himself, "an innocent and lovely boy? Why not I who have lived my life?"

David bore his illness with great courage, but it made his parents desperately sad when he said one day, "Dad, I wouldn't mind dying if I knew there was somewhere to go afterward."

Jim Johnston was not a religious man; in fact, he frankly admits that during the war he used to tease those of his army comrades who wore crucifixes, saying laughingly that it was a bit late to start praying!

But he did just that, and he and his wife asked for the protection of God's love for David.

Their prayer did not go unanswered.

Somehow the news of David's illness became widely known, and he was visited by many well-wishers, including Derek Nimmo and Katie Manning, whose hearts were so touched that they used to rush off to see David on every possible occasion between performances of the show in which they were appearing. And what was more, many of these people were praying for David as well and in some cases were encouraging whole congregations in churches to do the same.

It was then that Jim Johnston learned the meaning of the world "love." He saw it, so he says, in the faces of the nurses when he went to visit David; he felt it in the sympathy shown to him by everyone he met. The loving thought of so many people helped him and his wife to bear their terrible burden of sorrow.

David was allowed out of hospital to spend Christmas 1974 with his family. Time was growing shorter, but Jim Johnston prayed in his distress, "What must I do? Why not take me instead?"

Then one day, quite unexpectedly, his sister-in-law said to him, "What about Ted Fricker?"

"Well, what about him?" Jim asked curiously.

"He's a faith healer," she replied. "I know you don't believe in such things, but what have you and David got to lose?"

Jim was ready to clutch at any straw. "As you say, what have I got to lose? Could you fix up a meeting?"

And so it was arranged that Jim Johnston should bring David to be treated by me at Wyndham Place.

A year passed, and Christmas came around again. At last I was able to tell him, "David is all right now. His troubles are over."

Jim wrote me a beautiful letter of gratitude.

David still attends hospital for observation. "And so he should," wrote Jim, "if only to show them what can be achieved with Christ's help, and also, I would add, to give his parents a chance to say 'thank you' periodically to those beautiful people, be they specialists—doctors or nurses—who lavished their love and attention on him those desperate weeks."

Jim Johnston concluded with a paraphrase of his own which he wrote in all sincerity to express what he felt:

"And there came three wise men. The first from the East, offering his love and his care. The next from the Great Metropolis, bestowing the priceless gift of time, and lastly Ted Fricker, endowing us with hope, then charity, and finally the most important of all—a son restored to health."

This story serves to show the mysterious way in which everything in God's plan fits into the pattern of life.

At first, perhaps, it may appear to be a great injustice that an innocent child should have to suffer in this way, but his suffering served more than one purpose.

If David had not suffered, his father would not have learned the meaning of love through his own suffering, nor would he have come to know that sincere prayer to God can be answered.

David himself had learned to face death with fortitude and perhaps had been brought to realize that there is, in fact, somewhere to go when we die, for through the power of healing, God had shown him that He cared.

Not only this, but those who read this story may themselves learn something of God's purpose and of the existence of His healing power.

There is another story which shows how God's healing power can come to the aid of someone who has had to endure years of suffering, bravely borne.

Mrs. Pauline Canney had a busy practice in physiotherapy and osteopathy when she became ill and had to have a double gynecological operation.

After it was over, she was looking forward to a resumption of her work, but far from being able to do so, she found herself crippled and her life ruined.

There was a terrible feeling of tightness and stretching

inside the pelvis and lower abdomen, with continuous pain. Lying on her side in bed was impossible, and sitting brought on more pain and made her feel terribly ill.

All the functions of the pelvic organs were affected, and bowel action took place every half hour. The only position which was bearable and which gave relief was lying flat on her back, and for several years most of her life was spent in that position.

Eventually another operation was performed which granted her some relief, but she was still far from comfortable. A further investigation by operation showed that through prolonged damage severe contracture had taken place and nothing could be done.

This final operation unfortunately irritated the already damaged pelvic nerves, and once more she was obliged to lie flat on her back in bed.

There was no hope of recovery, and as she had no means of livelihood her doctor talked of her being registered as a disabled person.

But, as very often happens in such cases, she had a kind friend who took her in his car, lying flat in a reclining seat, and brought her to me.

After she arrived at the clinic and was helped into my room, I sat quietly for a few minutes until I was told to tell her that new tissue would be made to grow, but that it would take time, as all growth does.

Let Mrs. Canney tell her own story:

"Very gradually I improved until eventually I was able to make the long journey by train alone.

"In the early months of the healing I was woken up in the night by a strong electric-type current which went through me for one or two hours. As I got better, so this lessened.

"Only someone who has lost all hope of recovery and

whose life is unbearable can understand what it is to be able once again to make plans for the future and even just to walk out in the air. Through Mr. Fricker life was gradually given back to me, and still I am improving.

"Throughout the years of suffering I was upheld by some wonderful friends without whose help I could not even have traveled to Mr. Fricker.

"The healing I have had through him is a miracle, and I can never express how deep is my gratitude to God for His love in bringing me to such a wonderful healer."

I can only repeat that I am but the instrument, and the healing power is God's.

Death in this world is an experience through which we all have to pass at some time or other. It is not so terrible as most people imagine.

When the time is near for you to pass on, your closest relatives and friends are brought down to you in order to help you as you leave the body. Immediately after the silver cord which joins your spirit to your physical body is severed, you do not realize that any change has taken place, and you think that you are still alive on earth. To lessen the shock, your relatives come to you so that when you see them you will realize that you are indeed still alive, but in another world.

If you have ever been in the room when a person is dying, you will know that sometimes it appears that the dying person is wandering in his mind because he seems to be talking to people long since dead. But he is not wandering; he *is* actually talking to these people because his spirit is out of his body although still attached to it by the silver cord.

Everyone has in his mind what I term a "computer" which records every aspect of his life as he lives it. When he is being prepared to leave his body, he is shown this record as though on a film so that he can see and remember where he succeeded and where he strayed from the right path.

It is not a weighing of the soul against the feather of truth in order to determine his punishment. There is no punishment. The purpose is to explain to him that by the life he has led on this earth he has merited a new life on the level of a sphere in the other world which is appropriate to the state of evolution of his spirit.

It is explained to him that although he may go to a sphere which is perhaps below that of his loved ones who may have progressed in their evolution since leaving this earth, they are allowed to come down to visit him. But he may not ascend to their level until such time as he has advanced in his own evolution.

After the film of his life has been shown to him, the dying person is then told that the time has come for him to leave his body. The silver cord is severed; his spirit is released from the body; and in a split second he is no longer in the hospital or bedroom, but finds himself in the other world. The fact of this instantaneous transition from this world to the next is always a great source of wonder to me, because the sphere to which he goes in the spirit world is outside the physical universe, which is of unknown immensity.

I have been told by my Voice many things of this nature, and always their truth has been proved to me by a practical example. The foregoing statements are no exception.

One evening I got a telephone call from a friend who wanted my help. Now, I was instructed that I must work regularly between certain hours, just as most people do.

Outside these hours I was to lead my own private life. I have always made a practice of doing this, otherwise the strain would be intolerable.

This particular night was a Saturday, and the friend asked me if I would go down to the London Clinic where his brother-in-law was lying in a coma.

"I know he is past saving," he said, "but all the women there are dreadfully upset. If you could just talk to them a little about life after death, it would make them feel so much happier."

To my surprise, instead of saying no as I always did, I heard myself saying, "Yes, of course I'll come."

Then I thought, "My goodness, what have I done? My wife will not be very pleased with me for going out on a Saturday."

But it shows how God plans everything, because when I went in to tell my wife, expecting her to be rather annoyed, she simply said sweetly, "Of course you must go."

So off I went.

When I had found the room where the man was dying, I knocked on the door, which was opened by my friend, who thanked me for coming. As I entered the room, the brother-in-law, who had been lying in a coma, sat up in bed and shouted, "Who is Mr. Fricker? Who is Mr. Fricker? They tell me to hang on to Mr. Fricker. He is the only one who can help me!"

So I walked up to the bed and, taking his hand, I said to him gently, "Don't worry. I'll help you."

"Who is that big black man with you?" he cried out in agitation.

I always have a big Negro youth with me who is over seven feet tall. The dying man was seeing him with his spiritual eyes, because he was out of his body.

I said quietly, "It's a friend of mine. Don't be afraid."

Then he came back into his body again and said that they had told him I was the only one who could help him.

Then occurred the strangest four-dimensional conversation. His spirit kept on going outside his body and coming back with messages from the ones who were helping him. On one occasion he came back and said, "Mr. Fricker, why can I see my body in the bed while they are showing me the film of my life?"

I comforted him and told him that it would all be explained to him.

Here was the actual proof of what I had been told—that a dying man is shown a film of his life. It was clearly for this purpose that he had been allowed to come back and tell me about it.

After he had said this, I asked those helping him, "Why have you sent for me to come here?"

"This is a very unusual case," was the answer. "We cannot get his silver cord to snap. So we put the thought in your friend's mind to telephone you, and we also put the thought that you should agree to come into your mind and that of your wife. We need you to help us by putting enough power through his body to snap the silver cord."

I immediately did so, and he went.

I had been sent for, not to try and bring the man back but to help him to go.

I comforted the relatives and told them that he was now at peace. I could see that they were scared by what they had witnessed because they could not understand where the messages were coming from. I cannot say that I was surprised.

Having done all that I could to give them comfort, I said good-bye and left the room.

It must have been six months later that I was invited to

an engagement party, and who should be there but my friend and the six women relatives who had been in the dying man's room. As soon as they saw me they rushed up and started firing questions at me: "What was he talking to you about?" "How did he know who you were?" "Who was that black man?" And so on.

So then I explained at length to them what had happened, and they went away satisfied.

It is not only when a person is dying that his spirit can leave his body to visit the other world for a time and then return. I know that this happens very often to me during sleep because my Voice has told me so, but I have never been allowed to remember anything that took place.

There was one occasion when an exception was made. It happened like this.

Ever since I began healing, many people have come to me not only for the curing of some ailment but in order to ask advice about personal problems—either to do with family or business. None has gone away empty-handed.

I listen to what they have to tell me, and in some strange way it always seems that I am able to provide a solution. It has puzzled me for a long time how I have been able to give advice, particularly on business problems, using language and expressions which I myself did not understand. Often after giving advice I have thought to myself, "How on earth do I know all this?"

I knew that at night during sleep I used to go into the other world, but next morning I never remembered anything about it.

About two years ago I was talking one night with my spirit friends when I was suddenly told, "When you come up tonight, you will be allowed to remember what you see and what we tell you."

In excited anticipation I lay back and tried to sleep. What happened after that I shall never forget.

A spirit guide who had been sent down to help me made himself known to me, and I could hardly wait to ask him where we were going.

"We are going," he replied, "to see the place in which you will live when you finally come over to this world."

Immediately my curiosity was aroused, but he would tell me no more.

Now there are many fanciful stories about traveling to the so-called astral plane which give the impression of a long journey made by a kind of spiritual flight through space. There is no truth in this at all. I will tell you exactly what happened.

Having explained to me where he was taking me, the guide said, "Right, we're going now."

The next thing I knew was that I was standing outside the place he had told me about. My spirit had traveled from earth to the other world with the speed of thought. No journey through the stars in space—I was there in a flash.

I found myself standing outside a very large and beautiful house rather like a building upon earth, and yet there was something different about it which it is hard to describe. My guide explained to me that this was to be my home when I had left my life on earth.

I was allowed a few moments to survey the scene, and then my guide invited me to go inside.

We entered a very long room which seemed to me like a library, and at the very end were seated three old men with long white beards, just like Father Christmas.

Now I had always been led to believe that everyone in the spirit world looked in his prime—not a day over thirty. When I saw these three old men, I thought someone had been misleading me.

I am a very outspoken man, and I told my guide in no uncertain terms what I thought about this deception, using in the process some very descriptive expressions. "I thought nobody up here ever looked more than thirty," I said, "these ones look about a hundred!"

One of the old men—I can see him now—rose from his seat and approached me with a beaming smile on his face. When he came up to me, the guide, who appeared a bit shocked by my candid observations, started to apologize for me. "I told you what a terror he was," said the guide.

"No," replied the old man, "he's not a terror! We had him made this way. In the past we sent down so-called religious people, we sent 'do-gooders,' we sent all kinds—and it never worked. So we had a natural man made who would say exactly what he thought whether to a king or a beggar, and he's been successful at it! He's all right."

Turning to me, the old man said, "How can I explain to you why we look so old?"

He appeared to give the matter some consideration for a moment and then went on, "In your world, when a Shakespeare play is to be performed, the actors dress themselves up to suit the part they have to portray. Here it is the same. We are known as the Three Wise Men, and so we have to dress the part so that you will recognize who we are. But when we have finished what we have to do, then we cast off our role as Three Wise Men and appear once more as young men, just like all other people in the spirit world."

After he had said this, I asked him why I had been brought to see them.

"We have realized for some time," he replied, "that the things we have been doing to you have puzzled you again and again. So we thought it was time we gave you an explanation."

He paused and then continued, "What we do is this.

Each night we feed into your spirit's computer the answers to all the questions your patients are going to ask you the next day. If the patients have a great difficulty, we make them tell you about it. You will hear them say after, 'I wouldn't tell anyone else in the world, Mr. Fricker.' As soon as they have told you, the answer will come from you and you will tell them what to do."

"But," I objected, "sometimes people get held up in the traffic or cancel their appointments, so how can you possibly do this?"

"This is all planned out," said the old man. "We know exactly who is coming tomorrow and who is not. Nobody can get the wrong message."

When my spirit had returned to my body, I remembered all that had happened and what I had been told.

I spent most of the next day pondering upon the vastness of God's plan which numbers the very hairs of our head and does not allow one sparrow to fall to the ground without His knowledge.

There are other occasions when the spirit leaves the body and yet remains in the earth sphere without entering the spirit world.

For instance, there is a type of experience which is fairly common and can happen to anybody. Perhaps you may go on a motoring holiday to a district or country with which you are totally unfamiliar. As you are going along, a thought comes into your mind that a mile or two down the road there is a beautiful little church next to a farm. After a few minutes you come upon the very church you had seen in your imagination. Immediately you think to yourself, "How on earth did I know about that? I've never been here before!"

Then your mind seeks a rational explanation, and you

may hit upon the notion that you may have been born and lived there in a previous life on earth and that is why you remember it. But this is not so.

What really happens is that your spirit is taking such an interest in the journey that it travels in advance of your body down the road and brings back to you the thought in picture form of what it has seen.

Or, again, you may be walking down the street and you think you recognize a friend of yours a little way in front of you, but when you catch up to him you find you are mistaken. And yet, after continuing on a few hundred yards, to your surprise there is your friend waiting to cross the road. You find this extremely puzzling at the time, but the explanation is the same as before. Your spirit has been traveling in advance of your body and having encountered your friend it brings back to your mind the thought of him. The picture of him is so fresh in your mind that you are led into the error of imagining that the first person you see is none other than he.

There have been many cases reported of people who have been rendered unconscious in an accident and have experienced the strange sensation of looking down at their bodies from outside themselves. Where a person still has a span of life to complete, then the silver cord joining the spirit to the body remains intact and the spirit returns to the body when consciousness is regained. But in the case of those, perhaps involved in the same accident, whose time has come to pass on, the silver cord snaps and they can no longer return to their bodies.

Occasionally you may read of someone injured in an accident who has narrowly escaped death, and when he returns to consciousness he tells the strange story of how he has seen his past life flash before his eyes. This is, in fact, perfectly true, because what has happened is that the shock of the sudden accident has driven the spirit out of the body and triggered off the computer mechanism which shows him part of the film of his life, even though his time has not yet come to pass on to the other world.

This kind of incident helps to impress upon our minds the fact that we have two bodies, a physical body and a spirit body. The physical body is only a suit of clothes which is cast off when it is no longer required, but the spirit body lives on eternally.

Incidentally, something which has always puzzled me is how it happens that when relatives and friends who have passed over come back to me for the first time, they always show themselves in the clothes that they used to wear on earth so that I shall recognize them. These clothes may perhaps have been destroyed but appear to be exactly as they had been.

The sorts of experience which I have just related are completely involuntary, but it appears that scientific research is at present being carried on in order to discover if it is possible for the spirit to leave the physical body of its own volition as there are reports of evidence showing that this has, in fact, been done.

8

A Gift from Elizabeth

I am not a spiritualist, and up to the time that I started using my healing gift I knew nothing of spiritualism except for my experience with the medium Joseph Benjamin, who first told me of my healing mission, and with Mrs. Turner, who confirmed it in the little tin church.

But there was an occasion when I became involved quite unintentionally in a spiritualist séance.

After I had been healing for three or four years, a friend of mine came to me one day and told me that he had had a most unusual experience. He had been to a séance at which trumpets had been used for receiving communications from people in the other world.

It was his first experience of this kind, and he had been able to talk to his wife, who had passed on a year previously. She was German, and the whole of their conversation had been carried on in German. He had asked her questions in German, and she had answered through the trumpet in the same lanugage. They had discussed personal matters about which nobody in the room could possibly have had any knowledge.

He was so impressed by the medium that he asked him if he would come to his house and hold a séance there.

He told me he had just had a letter from the medium agreeing to come in a month's time.

My friend confessed himself to be rather nervous about this and asked me if I would like to come and perhaps give him a little moral support.

I demurred, protesting that I really had no knowledge of such things, but in the end in order to please him I agreed to go.

He said that he would fetch me on my free afternoon and we would go together to his house and decide on a suitable room where we could ensure that the séance could be held under test conditions. He had invited ten friends to attend also, none of whom had any experience of communication by trumpet and who were completely unknown to the medium.

When the medium arrived no introductions were made by name, which was a procedure agreeable to the medium, who was quite willing to work under test conditions. The medium asked if he could have ten minutes to relax in the room before the séance began. This would help to build up power.

After he had done this, my friend and I went back into the room for a final examination and found things satisfactory.

Then we all trooped into the room and took our places. I sat next to the wife of a friend, and on her other side was the medium.

Amid a great air of expectancy from the sitters, the medium's wife placed two trumpets treated with luminous paint on a table in the center of the circle. About twenty-five feet away, she put a record player, which provided soft music in the background. The lights in the room were then switched off, and the room was in darkness except for the red light on the record player.

A short time after the medium had gone into a deep trance state, one of the trumpets rose into the air and a voice introduced himself to us as the medium's guide. He explained to us that when this particular trumpet rose up, it would be for him to speak to us and to answer any of our questions. But if the other trumpet rose into the air, it would be for a relative or friend of one of the sitters to speak through, or if there was another medium or healer present,their guides would speak to them through it.

Now, my friend was the only person who knew that I was a healer, and he had told nobody. At that time I had not been working for long and was as yet not very well known. The séance was held in Surrey, and my clinic was in north London, so it was extremely unlikely that anyone in the room would have heard of me.

After we had been given instructions by the guide, the trumpet returned to the table. A few seconds later, the other trumpet rose right up to the ceiling, and through it a voice called, "Don't you recognize me? It's Sambo."

Not only by the name but also by the voice I knew that it was my Negro boy who is always with me, and in order to dispel any doubt I might have had, he mentioned to me something he had said three days before. This was to me complete proof that it was he.

The trumpet descended, only to rise again, and this time the voice of Dr. Muller, who advises me on spinal cases, spoke to me about a case we had worked on a few days previously.

He was followed by another doctor, Abdal Latif, who reminded me of a case of cancer we had recently treated.

Then I had a most happy experience, for the next voice to speak was that of my mother, who came to tell me how pleased she was that I was using my healing gift to help the sick. I have no doubt whatsoever that it was she.

After the second trumpet had settled back onto the table, the first trumpet came up again and the medium's guide inquired if there was anything we wanted to ask.

There was a young girl about seventeen years old who answered that she would like to talk to her friend Elizabeth. The guide said that he would do his best, but there were a great many people waiting to talk and the only thing he could do was to call out "Elizabeth!" and hope that the right person came through.

Then through the second trumpet the beautiful voice of a woman spoke, saying, "I am Elizabeth," and the young girl called out to her. But it was not her friend, for the trumpet suddenly flew across the room and started hitting me on the chest, which scared me out of my wits.

Through the trumpet the beautiful voice said to me, "I am your Aunt Elizabeth."

This for me was something of an anticlimax, for I knew of no Aunt Elizabeth and said as much. But the voice insisted that she was my aunt and said that one day I would discover that this was so.

However, she told me that the purpose of her coming was to let me know that she was going to send me a beautiful oil painting of a bowl of old-fashioned roses. She asked me to keep it in my healing room at the clinic, which I promised to do. Determined to make my point, I once again said that I was sure that I had no Aunt Elizabeth. With equal persistence she assured me that one day I would find out.

After that, some of the sitters received a few more messages, and the séance came to an end.

The following week, I was working in my clinic in Tottenham when there was a knock on the door. When I opened it, there stood on the doorstep a railway employee whom I had known well as a boy at school.

He said, "I've got a parcel here for you," and produced

a package sewn up in sackcloth with a label addressed to "Fricker, Tottenham."

"You can't sign for it," he said, "because it's not on my list. I know you are the only Fricker in Tottenham, so it must be for you."

I took the parcel from him and, consumed with curiosity, removed the wrapping and withdrew the contents. It was an oil painting of a bowl of old-fashioned roses, exactly as my alleged Aunt Elizabeth had described.

As soon as I could, I rang up the railway office and asked them if they could trace the sender of the parcel which I had received that morning by railway delivery. The clerk searched his books and said that, as far as he could see, I had not received any parcel that morning, for there was no record of it at all.

There was only one thing I could do—I sent the picture to be framed and then hung it on the wall of my healing room as I had promised.

It was still hanging upon the wall seven years later when a young man came to me with spinal trouble.

I treated him once and told him that I thought he would have no further trouble but that I would like to check it in a week's time. He returned on the appointed day, and I found that he was all right.

He thanked me and said, "I never thought I would have to come to a cousin to have this cured."

"Cousin?" I said. "But I don't even know you."

He then said how his mother had told him all about his family, and what he told me left me in no doubt at all that he was my cousin.

Then it struck me that he might be able to tell me if we had ever had an Aunt Elizabeth.

"Oh yes," he said, "she died about thirty-seven years ago."

I questioned him about her and asked where she had

lived. It turned out that her home had been situated about five hundred yards from the house in Surrey where she had spoken to me at the séance.

A week after the young man had told me all this, my Aunt Elizabeth came through to me. She told me that the picture had been wrapped up in sacking and left in the attic of her home, and she was afraid that it might be thrown out as rubbish when the attic was being cleared. So she had decided to send it to me as it was a beautiful picture of which she was very fond.

As a tribute to her I have named the picture "Elizabeth," but to this day it remains a mystery how it was sent to me, addressed to Tottenham with my name on it.

I myself always wear the Christian symbol in the form of a gold ring with a raised cross upon it.

It happened one day that I was told by my Voice that I must have made a heavy gold ring of eighteen-carat gold. On it there was to be a gold cross in relief, and I was shown exactly what it was to look like. So that I should remember, I made a sketch of the design.

I took this sketch to six different jewelers, but none would take on the job. I know now that this was all part of a plan, but at the time I was rather annoyed and decided to forget about the whole thing.

Two or three months later, I was taken to task by my Voice and was asked why I had not yet had the ring made. I explained that I had tried six jewelers without any result. I was then told that somebody would be sent to me.

This was on a Friday morning. On the following Monday I was giving someone healing for the first time, and as I was chatting with him I asked what he did for a living.

"I'm a goldsmith," he said. "My principal job is

making gold rings for the bishops and clergy of the church."

It quickly came into my mind that this must be the person they had promised to send to me. "Tell me," I said, "would you like to make me a ring?"

He said that he would, and so I described to him the kind of ring that I wanted, stressing that it must be very heavy and made of eighteen-carat gold.

He said that he would like to make it for me, but that eighteen-carat gold was hard to come by, and as my order was not in the ordinary line of business, he would not be able to stamp it for me with a gold mark. I said that I only wanted it for my work and I did not mind if it was marked or not.

When he finished the ring he brought it to me, and I saw that it was a beautiful piece of work. I looked inside and noted that there was no gold mark as I had expected. He saw me do this and hastened to assure me that it was indeed eighteen-carat gold.

About two months later, Christmas was approaching, and we set up our usual Christmas trees at home—one in the hall and one outside on the doorstep.

One evening when I returned home from work, I was met by my wife at the door, who told me that the electric lamps on the tree outside the door kept on flickering on and off, and she asked me to try and fix them. Thinking that it must be a loose electric bulb, I went outside to see what I could do. It was a beautiful moonlit night with an exceptionally clear sky for the time of year.

I am very nervous about electricity, so before I went out I made sure that the electric plug was pulled out of its socket. I then tried each lamp in turn to see if any of them were making loose connections.

Suddenly there was a terrific flash like lightning out of

the sky which hit my ring directly. The pain in my finger was excruciating, and thinking that someone must have put the plug back in again, I said in no uncertain terms what I thought about it.

My wife came running out to me, and I cried out, "I'm in agony! I've been struck by lightning!"

"Don't be silly!" she said. "Lightning on a night like this?"

I was in such pain that I pulled the ring off my finger and, for some reason, glanced inside.

"My God!" I exclaimed. "That lightning has made a mark inside my ring!" To my naked eye, it looked like a gold mark.

A few weeks went by, and one night my Voice said to me, "You did not see what we did to your ring, did you?"

"Yes, I did," I said, "you put a gold mark inside it."

"Look again," I was told, "this time with a magnifying glass."

I fetched a magnifying glass and had a close look at the mark inside the ring.

It was a crown of thorns.

My Voice then told me that this was only the second time in the history of the world that such a thing had ever been done.

The first time was on Mount Sinai when Moses was given the two tablets of stone containing the Ten Commandments "written with the finger of God."

Christmas often seems to be the time when strange things happen to me.

I once had a woman patient who was an amateur painter. She asked me if she could paint my picture, and I gave her a photograph from which to work.

When the picture was finished she brought it to me,

and I saw that she had painted a figure of me in the foreground, and in the background were two frameless windows through which the blue sky was visible. In the left-hand window was painted a crucifix, but the right-hand window was clear blue sky.

I accepted it with pleasure and hung it on my wall in such a position that it could be seen in a mirror facing my chair.

One day I was sitting there when I chanced to look up and thought I noticed something different about the picture which I could see in the mirror. I looked again more carefully and realized that the right-hand window, which had previously been light blue, had changed in color and was now much darker than the other one.

Continuing to stare at it, I could see the misty outline of the face of Jesus in profile.

Perhaps because it was nearly Christmas I was being shown that as a follower of Jesus I was not forgotten.

I call it my "miracle" picture.

9

Sambo, My Friend and Bodyguard

As I have said before, this world is a training ground for the spirit. During the course of our life here, we are set a number of problems in the solving of which our spirit can learn certain lessons. Every lesson we learn advances the evolution of our spirit toward a higher state of development, and in time our spirit will have advanced sufficiently to be reborn on some other planet in the universe where existence is on a higher level.

If we fail to learn our lesson for some reason, then we shall probably have to return once again to this world where the same problem will be put to us again. There is no punishment for not passing our examination, we simply continue to return to this world until we have finally mastered the problem and can go on to better things. Nobody can learn everything in one short span of life, and those of us who are here now must certainly have been here before. There is some small consolation in the fact that we cannot go any lower than we are now, for this earth is the lowest plane of existence for the human spirit.

The only place which might be termed as a lower plane of existence is the nameless darkness where the earth-bound spirits exist. They are the spirits of those who have committed suicide on earth hoping to escape the unpleasant consequence of some act or simply because they have not the courage to live out their lives here. Since they have cut short their allotted span of life in the world, they are obliged to live the remainder of it in a state of limbo between this earth and the other world.

But not all suicides suffer in this way. God is merciful and takes into account all extenuating circumstances, as, for instance, when the balance of a person's mind has been disturbed and he cannot be held fully responsible for his actions.

Many people when under extreme pressure or in a state of acute depression have been assailed by a terrible urge to take their own lives. I cannot stress too strongly that if ever such a thought should occur to anybody, he should immediately phone a friend, or if no friend is available, then get in touch with the Samaritans and tell them about it. By making contact in this way with another human being, the spell will be broken and tragedy averted.

I have sometimes been sent into this outer darkness to rescue an earthbound spirit whose time has come to move on to another plane of existence. When this happens I have to wear a kind of cloak to cover my aura, which would otherwise shine so brightly in the darkness that the earthbound spirit would be completely dazzled and unable to see me.

It is these earthbound spirits which can be a great danger to anyone using a Ouija board or some similar form of attempted communication. The contacts made in this way are with earthbound spirits who are sometimes able to touch the aura of the experimenter and pass on to him the mental condition which led to the act of suicide. Anyone indulging in this form of experiment is extremely vulnerable, and it should never be undertaken for any reason at all.

Other manifestations of earthbound spirits are encountered in some houses where objects have been smashed and thrown about and all manner of disturbance has taken place. There is no intention to harm people physically; it is more of an attempt by the earthbound spirit to draw attention to itself because of the frustration it experiences in not being able to communicate with, or be seen by, the occupants of the house.

This is a subject in which people should never dabble. I am protected from these harmful influences by my constant companion Sambo, who acts as my guardian and is able to drive away from me any earthbound spirit which might attempt to approach.

I will tell you a story in a less serious vein about Sambo.

Sambo is a great friend of myself and my family, although I am the only one who can see him. He not only guards me but is most helpful in all sorts of small ways. For instance, if my wife is driving in London and cannot find a place to park her car, she will ask Sambo to help, and in some extraordinary way he always finds a place for her.

He is also a great finder of lost property, and on more than one occasion has obliged a patient by locating something which could not be found.

One of my patients lost a watch of great sentimental value, and as I could see she was very upset, I asked Sambo if he could find it for her.

"Tell her to look in the right-hand drawer of the chest of drawers in her room," said Sambo at once. "She will find it there under some clothes."

And she did.

On another occasion she rang me again. "I'm in great trouble, Mr. Fricker," she said in an agitated voice. "My brother's car has been stolen, and there are some very important papers in a briefcase inside it."

While she was telling me this, Sambo said, "Tell her not to worry. I have found the car and I have pushed the briefcase under the back seat where nobody can see it. The car was taken by two boys for a joyride, and when he finds it the briefcase will be there."

To his relief her brother found the briefcase in the car under the back seat exactly as Sambo had said.

Six months later, she rang me a third time with another tale of woe. She told me that she had been having a bath, and afterward her engagement ring had slipped from her finger as she was cleaning the tub. The ring disappeared down the drain! The previous occasion when she could not find her watch, it was probably just mislaid. But this time the ring was in a totally inaccessible place, and I did not see how Sambo could possibly find it.

But Sambo was quite undaunted by the situation. "Tell her she is to go to bed," he said, "and in the morning when she wakes up she will find it on the carpet in the bathroom."

Not without misgiving, I gave her the message. I need not have worried. The next morning she found the ring on the bathroom carpet!

Not very long ago another woman patient told me she had lost a very expensive watch which her husband had given her.

Sambo must have been listening because he told me to ask her if she had been handling any clothes recently. I asked her this, and she replied that she had been doing charitable work and had been collecting some dresses for this purpose.

"Tell her it caught in the clothes and fell off. It will be found," said Sambo.

She rang up the man from whose flat she had collected the dresses, but he had gone away for a few days. After he returned, she got in touch with him and asked if he had found a watch.

"Oh, yes," he said, "I found it just before I went away, and put it in my pocket as I was in too much of a hurry to find out whose it was. I think it's still there. Hang on a minute."

A moment later, he returned to the telephone. "I've got it," he said. "I'll send it around to you."

She was delighted and asked me to thank Sambo.

Sometime later, she came to see me and asked me somewhat apologetically to help her again. This time she had lost a ring. "Could you please ask Sambo to find it?" she said tentatively.

"Of course," I replied.

"She lost it when she took her gloves off," said Sambo at once.

I told her what he had said, and, thinking back, she remembered that two evenings before, she had been wearing her ring and had taken off her gloves on returning home.

"I've got them here now," she exclaimed. But a search revealed nothing.

Sambo told me to tell her to go home and look at the place where she had taken off her gloves and she would find the ring lying on the carpet.

Two minutes after arriving home she was on the telephone to me. "Ted," she said, "I've found it. It was lying on the edge of the carpet, just as Sambo said!"

On another occasion a friend of mine who is well known to Sambo went shopping in order to get a new rubber ring for his vacuum cleaner. He went from shop to shop, but nowhere could he find a ring of the required size.

In a state of frustration he finally decided to go home without it. On opening the door of his car, what should he see on the floor but a rubber ring which proved to fit his vacuum cleaner exactly.

It was a small thing, but just another example of Sambo's thoughtfulness.

Sambo is extremely kind and helpful to anyone who asks his help not only in finding things but in solving people's problems. If he does not know the answer himself, he will always find someone who does, and the thought will be put into the mind of the person who has asked his help.

Sambo is my personal bodyguard and is always close to me. He was once an African slave but is now a shining spirit in the other world.

There was an occasion when a woman rang me up to say that her sister in America was ill and had telephoned to ask if I could give her any help.

"Tell her to think of me by name," I said, "and I will give her absent healing."

The sister had not met me personally but had heard of me.

Two days later, the woman was on the telephone again, sounding slightly bewildered.

"Mr. Fricker," she said, "I've had a cable from my sister in America. It says: 'Stop absent healing.' "

"That's peculiar," I said, thinking that perhaps the sister did not believe that I could help her.

"I'm ringing her tonight," said the woman. "I'll let you know what it's all about."

True to her promise, she telephoned me at the first opportunity.

It appeared that the sister had done as I suggested and was quietly concentrating on me when suddenly she felt the presence of someone in front of her.

"I looked up," said the sister, "and there, standing in front of me, I saw a black man about seven feet tall. I got the fright of my life. Then he spoke to me and said, "Don't worry, gel, we'll fix you up!' [Sambo picks up these slang expressions from me, I'm afraid to say.] Then I must have fainted," went on the sister, "but in the morning when I woke up, I was completely cured."

The sister in America had no knowledge of Sambo's existence, so she was understandably startled by his unexpected appearance.

It may seem strange that Sambo could be in America and yet guard me at the same time. But it is not really so, for distance means nothing in the other world, and a spirit can travel to any part of the world and back with the speed of thought.

I am sure that my wife, Grace, will forgive me if I tell a little story concerning Sambo which still gives rise to mirth within the family.

As I have said, I am the only one of the family who can see Sambo in spite of the fact that we think of him as one of us.

One day my wife expressed a wish to see Sambo for herself. Now, Sambo will never show himself to anyone if he thinks that this might cause the person to be alarmed by such an unusual occurrence. So I said to her, "Are you sure you won't be frightened?"

"Oh, no," she replied indignantly. "Of course I won't be afraid of Sambo. I know him so well."

Sambo, of course, heard these remarks but said nothing.

One evening a little while afterward, my daughter Theresa and I were watching television, and Grace announced that she was tired. She said goodnight to us and went up to bed.

A few minutes later, we heard the sound of rushing footsteps descending the stairs at full speed. The door burst open. It was Grace in a state of great agitation. When she had calmed down a little, I asked her what on earth was wrong.

"It's Sambo," she managed to say at last. "I saw him!"

Then she told us what had happened.

She had gone upstairs into her dressing room and had started to get ready for bed. Suddenly her attention was drawn to something in the corner of the room. It was a pair of black legs! She became rooted to the spot and could not drag her eyes away from this remarkable sight. Gradually more of Sambo's body built up by slow stages until all but his neck and head had appeared. At this point she could bear no more and turned and fled out of the room and down the stairs.

Because he does not want to frighten her, Sambo has not shown himself to her again, but for a long time afterward Grace refused to go upstairs by herself to bed.

Grace herself is an extremely gifted healer.

Soon after I started my healing mission, I was besieged by hundreds of sick people seeking relief from their ailments who used to stand in a queue in the street outside my clinic.

The pressure became so great that one day I said to my Voice, "I shall never be able to cope with all these people on my own. You'll have to send me some help."

"You must get your wife to help you," was the answer.

"But she has no idea how to do this," I objected.

"Well, we shall have to give her the power to heal," said my Voice, "and she will be able to give you the assistance you need. Encourage her to come into your room and try it, and we will convince her that she can do it."

I waited for a time, and then one day I suggested that she should come and try her hand at healing as I had been told that she had been given the power so that if I had to be away from the clinic or became ill she would be able to take over for me until I returned.

"I don't know if I could do that," she said.

"Well, come in anyway and try," I urged her.

In the end, she allowed herself to be persuaded.

In order that she could see the results of her efforts, I chose a spinal case because such cases are more susceptible to rapid cure. I showed her what to do and told her to relax and the thought would be put into her mind by my helpers so that she would know where to place her hands. As she was not able to hear my Voice, my helpers would guide her in this way.

After she had treated the man, I examined him and found that his spine was completely all right. I made him take off his brace and come back to do various exercises to show my wife that she had, in fact, cured him.

The patient left the room, and I saw Grace looking doubtful.

"I'm not sure it was I that cured him," she said doubtfully. "I believe you did it when you shook hands with him as he came into the room."

Her misgivings were quite understandable.

"All right," I said, "let's wait a bit and then I'll get another patient, and this time I promise not to go anywhere near him." I was determined to convince her.

After I had treated a few more cases, another spinal

patient came in wearing a brace. I left the patient entirely to her, and when she had finished I was able to see without touching him that he was cured. I asked him to go outside and take off his corset and then to come back and let my wife see what movements he could perform.

I asked him what action he found the most difficult.

"I could never bend right over," he said.

"Right," I told him. "Bend over and touch your toes."

He did this and then sat down in the armchair, for he had had great difficulty in getting out of the chair. This he did successfully.

As a final proof I asked him if there was anything else that he had been unable to do.

"Yes," he answered, "I could never get out of bed properly."

"Well, I'm sorry," I said, "we haven't a bed here, so you'd better lie on the floor and try to get up from there, which is much more difficult."

So he lay down, and, after turning his body from side to side, he sat up and finally jumped to his feet without any trouble at all.

Grace was at last convinced by this, and it gave her confidence in her power to heal.

She became so successful at healing people that I had not the slightest hesitation in letting her take my place when I had to go away, and she was the only person except for one other whom I could confidently leave in charge. This is still so today.

Not only does she stand in for me, but she also goes out to visit the bedridden and patients too ill to come to the clinic. This is a wonderful work which she carries out lovingly and with great success.

I recently received a letter from Mrs. Jean Johnston, who was one of Grace's patients.

She had, in fact, made an appointment to see me, but I was away at that time and Grace was in charge. She described her feelings on the day she came to the clinic.

"I arrived in pain, depressed with the misery of endless nights without sleep. As I sat in the waiting room, my heart sank even lower when I discovered that you were not in attendance and I was to see 'a lady.'

"The lady introduced herself as 'Mrs. Fricker.' "

She proceeded to describe her symptoms and found a sympathetic listener in Grace, who then started to give her healing and discovered that she was suffering from spinal trouble.

After a few moments of gentle rubbing, the pain left her back and she felt a sensation of pins and needles in her left leg, which had been numb for almost a year.

"I was immediately able to bend and touch my toes," she said. "Only one more visit was necessary to help the muscles in my leg."

She admitted to being a doubter of the reality of healing power, but it seemed that she had a friend who with much patience had overcome Mrs. Johnston's reluctance to come to the clinic.

"An apology for my ignorance and doubt would seem useless," she said. "Words cannot express my gratitude to Mrs. Fricker."

This, of course, is only one instance of the many occasions on which Grace has successfully acted as my deputy.

The only other person in whose power I have complete confidence is a very great friend, Reginald Breary, whom I told a good many years ago that he had the gift of healing. He was a businessman of considerable standing, and yet after I told him of his power he used to come down to my clinic at every opportunity and help me in my work. So much so that I said to him that I feared his business would suffer. His only answer was: "This work of healing is far more important than business!"

Not only was he a good healer, but he was a man of the most happy disposition. This can be a very valuable asset to a healer because many patients are feeling miserable when they come for treatment and the effect of meeting a cheerful personality is an excellent tonic.

My wife and he are the only two people whom I feel I can safely leave to carry on my work while I am away.

Fortunately, he has somehow continued to keep his business going successfully at the same time.

My son, Derek, is the only one of my family who has not been directly involved in my healing work all these years, for the simple reason that he has made a career for himself and his family. He has been very successful in his chosen profession of architect, and I am delighted that this should be so.

In spite of his busy life, he has found time to send me many of his friends as patients, but beyond this he has not had the time to gain further knowledge of the work of healing.

You can imagine my surprise when, one Saturday morning when I called at his home as I was passing by, he quite unexpectedly said to me, "Dad, could I come and watch you doing healing one day?"

"Of course you can," I replied, "but whatever makes you say that?"

"Well," he said, "a few months ago I was at a party, and one of my friends hurt his back. So, just as a joke, I said to him, 'Come on! Let me do what my father does, and I'll fix you up!"

So he put his hands on his friend, and to his amazement it worked.

As a result of this, several more of his friends had come to him and asked him to treat their various ailments, which he did with success.

"I'd like to find out if I'm doing it properly," he went on, "so I thought I would ask you if I could come and see you at work."

One day in his spare time he came down to my clinic and watched me.

It so happened that that morning a patient came to me who was also a friend. He was suffering from spinal trouble, and I said to Derek, "Come and try it out. Don't worry if it doesn't work, because I will treat him afterward."

But it did work, and nobody was more pleased than I was to find that my son, in fact, had the gift of healing which I had always believed but about which I had never spoken to him.

This was only an experiment, but I now feel that God is preparing him to carry on the work when I have gone to the other world.

In my own case it took many years for God to prepare me for my healing mission, and it may be ten or even twenty years before Derek is ready, but meanwhile he can develop his gift by treating any friends who come to him.

If one day Derek is told that the time has come for him to carry on the work, it will make me very happy.

But this is a matter which only God can decide.

Occasionally I like to go abroad with Grace for a complete change from work, and on one such holiday I went to Cyprus. It was the first time I had been there, and I stayed in a lovely hotel on the beach near Famagusta.

Everyone needs rest sometimes, and when on holiday I try not to publish the fact; otherwise, I am likely to be besieged by hundreds of sick people whose requests for help I find it impossible to refuse.

However, on this particular holiday I did not remain incognito for long because I received a telephone call from a well-known osteopath who had somehow heard that I was staying there. He said he would be passing my hotel that morning on his way to a social engagement and wondered if he could come and have a word with me. I could not do otherwise than invite him to have a drink, and shortly afterward he arrived. We had an interesting discussion until the time came for him to go on his way.

When he had gone, a man came up to me in the casual way that people do when on holiday. He offered me a drink and then asked me, "Did I hear your name correctly? Are you Mr. Fricker?"

After I acknowledged that I was, he said to me, "Are you *the* Mr. Fricker?"

"It depends what you mean," I said warily.

"I mean Mr. Fricker the healer," he replied.

Again I said that this was so.

"I am a doctor," he told me, "and my practice is not far from your clinic in Tottenham."

I asked him not to disclose my name to anybody else as I was having a much-needed holiday, and he immediately understood that I did not want to be disturbed.

I am not a fanatical sightseer, and when on holiday I prefer to relax on a beach and just be generally lazy.

After lunch that day I was preparing to have a quiet afternoon when the same doctor came up and asked if I would like to visit a monastery about a mile down the road. This was the last thing I wanted to do, but to please him I agreed to go.

"I don't suppose we shall see many monks," he said, "they'll all be having a siesta."

"Lucky monks!" I thought to myself.

However, I tried to make the best of it and managed to push from my mind the vision of a luxurious afternoon on the beach in the warm sunshine.

Eventually we arrived at the monastery to find that his surmise had been correct and no monks were to be seen. But my friend proved an interesting and well-informed guide as he had been there several times. He was in the middle of telling me about three brothers who had been senior monks for a generation when he broke off and, pointing toward some steps, exclaimed, "Look, there's one of the monks!"

Turning around, I saw the figure of an old man about eighty years of age with a long white beard who was shuffling along with the aid of two sticks, his body bent almost double.

After five minutes or so, the old man came and stood in front of me and, looking up with difficulty, said, "Can you help me? My back is in a terrible condition."

"You mean the doctor," I said, indicating my friend.

"No," he replied, "I mean you."

I was astonished but unable to resist his appeal for help. Knowing what was likely to happen, I stretched out my hand and lightly touched his back. But the result surprised even me, for without warning he straightened up like a jack-in-the-box. Throwing away his sticks, he ran down the steps.

My friend looked at me accusingly. "You said you'd never been here before."

"I never have," I replied. "I have never even been in Cyprus before."

"If I hadn't seen it with my own eyes, I would never

have believed it!" said the doctor. "I have been coming here for years, and that monk I know to be a cripple, and yet there he is, running like a child."

Five minutes later the monk returned bearing in his hands two apples which he offered to me in gratitude for healing his spine. I was never more deeply touched.

Afterward my Voice told me that I had been guided to the monastery for the special purpose of healing this crippled monk. He had been asleep when I arrived, but my helpers had woken him up and told him that I was there to cure him. They had then let him see the light of my aura so that he would recognize me.

Two days later I returned to see how he was getting on. I was discussing the matter with his brothers, who were curious to know how the crippled monk had let me know that he wanted my help.

"He just spoke to me," I said.

"In your own language?" they inquired.

"Of course," I replied.

"But he does not speak a word of English!" they exclaimed in amazement.

"Well, he did two days ago," was my answer.

I was then invited to take wine with the monks. We repaired to the refectory and sat down at a long table where cups were placed before us. It was then that I received another surprise. The wine turned out to be Pepsi-Cola!

I returned to Cyprus several times, and whenever I visited the monastery I was greeted like a long-lost brother.

It was an experience which I shall never forget, and I never regretted giving up my lazy afternoon on the beach.

Some years ago when my clinic was still in Tottenham, I was visited by a well-known art expert who had come over from Holland to see me. He was suffering from serious osteoarthritis in the spine, but after only one healing treatment I was able to tell him to pack up his two sticks and go home.

News of his complete cure soon spread around Holland, and many patients came to me from there.

There was one very large firm which used to pay the fares of any of their staff members who were sick, and I would treat them and send them back healed.

The owner told me that it paid him to do this; otherwise, half of them would not be working. But in this way he could keep them all at work at the same time.

People come to me from all over the world for healing excepting from the Communist countries. I have had patients not only from Holland but also Switzerland, Denmark, Belgium, Spain, Portugal, France, Germany, and Finland. Many have come from the United States, South America, Australia, and South Africa. Thousands more patients I have never seen, but they know my name and have received absent healing.

A few years ago I was chatting to a friend one day when he mentioned that he and his wife wanted to go for a holiday to Italy. He asked my advice about where to go, and I recommended a very good hotel in a seaside resort I knew of. After hearing my description of it he finally decided to go.

When he returned he got in touch with me, and having said how much they had enjoyed the trip, he said that he had a very strange story to tell me.

It so happened that one fine morning he and his wife

were taking a stroll along the seafront of this resort in Italy, when his wife complained of a very severe headache.

As he knew all about absent healing, he said to her, "Why don't you think about Ted while we're walking, and maybe your headache will get better?"

They continued their walk, and as the light was perfect, he decided to take a picture of his wife with the movie camera which he always carried on holiday.

His wife had taken his advice and was slowly walking along, concentrating her mind on me in the hope of relieving her headache, while he was taking a moving picture of her from a short distance.

It was a good moment to take it as there was nobody else anywhere near her at the time.

When they returned home he had the film developed and, as all holiday makers do, he gave a party for some of his friends with a film show as well.

The camera shot of his wife on the seafront was sandwiched between other incidents, but when it was reached he saw to his amazement not only his wife strolling along but also an excellent picture of myself walking behind her!

Immediately the audience commented, "We didn't know Mr. Fricker was with you!"

"He wasn't with us," replied my friend.

"But he's there in the film," they insisted.

The whole thing seemed quite incredible to him because he knew perfectly well that I was in London at the time—as indeed I was—and he was certain that when he took the picture the seafront in the vicinity of his wife was devoid of people.

The only thing he omitted to tell me was whether his wife's headache got better!

All this may sound very strange to you, but there are hundreds of people who tell me that when they think of me at night they can see me in their room—so perhaps it is not really so unusual at all.

10

Katie Boyle and Other Case Histories

About thirteen years ago I received a telephone call from the husband of Katie Boyle, the famous television and radio star. She had been for some time in a Harley Street nursing home with a spinal injury that was the result of an accident. He told me that the BBC had received such a large number of messages from well-wishers mentioning my name that he had decided to ask if I could help her.

"Can you do anything for her?" he said. "I am desperate because the doctors have just told me that they can do nothing more. They've put a brace on her neck and shoulders and told her that she'll probably have to learn to live with the pain. I've brought her back home now, but she's obviously in agony and no drug seems to relieve it. As a last resort I'm asking you to help."

I replied that I would do anything I could for her and suggested that he should bring her down to me at once.

When she arrived she was crying with pain, and as I took her and her husband into my room, she said to me, "You know, Mr. Fricker, I have absolutely no faith in this sort of healing."

"Don't worry," I assured her, "you don't have to have any. I have enough faith for both of us."

Her left arm was partially paralyzed, and she was quite unable to lift it.

I placed my hands on the top of her spine at the back of her neck, and soon I could see that several of the vertebrae were displaced and had suffered severe damage.

In a few minutes, as I watched, the vertebrae moved back into their correct position and the damage healed up completely. I was then told to tell her to shake hands with her husband.

"Oh, but I can't do that," she said.

"Yes, you can!" I urged her.

With an effort of will, she raised her left arm and shook hands with him.

I had removed the brace from her neck in order to treat her, and I told her to turn her head from side to side. Gaining confidence, she once again found that she could do as I asked.

Her joy and excitement knew no bounds when she realized that she no longer had to face the dreadful prospect of wearing a brace permanently and suffering continuous and probably ever-increasing pain.

She had come in with tears of sadness, and she went out with tears of joy.

Just to reassure herself, she went at once to have an X-ray photograph taken, which showed that her spine was perfect.

From that day she has never had any further doubts about the power of healing, and she has sent me hundreds of patients from all walks of life. If, for instance, she is going down the street and sees a flower seller on a corner who is sick and in need of help, she will at once bring him to me for healing.

She is a charming person of sweet character, completely devoid of false pride. As I do, she regards all people as God's children and worthy of her help, whoever they may be and however humble or exalted their station.

One of the patients whom Katie Boyle sent to me was Pete Murray, the actor, disc jockey, and well-known BBC personality.

He had always had trouble with his back, but it had become much worse and he had to wear a plaster cast for support.

Then one day he dislodged something in his back so severely that he could scarcely walk. This was disastrous as he had to do a show for the BBC and the pain was so great that he doubted his ability to manage it.

It so happened that Katie Boyle, whom he knew well, had agreed to appear on the show in place of Pete Murray's original guest, who had been unable to come.

As soon as she saw him come in limping and obviously in pain, she announced that she was going to take him straight off to see me.

When he arrived I put my hands on him and realized what was wrong with his back. I treated him for a few minutes and then told him to stand straight up. He was not sure that he could, but he made the effort and to his surprise discovered that he had no pain. From that time, his back has been quite all right.

I have learned that it is not just by coincidence that people are brought to me for healing. They are guided to me by those in the other world because they are in need of help, and I am sure that it was not just by chance that Katie Boyle was at the BBC studio for Pete Murray's show on that day.

Another patient brought to me by Katie Boyle was Frances Bennett, the star of stage and television. Hers turned out to be one of those cases which give me special pleasure, not only because she is a charming person but also because her complete and immediate cure occurred three days before Christmas. As I have said, the nicest things seem to happen to me around about Christmas, and I look on them as my present from the other world.

She had been appearing for the BBC in a serial called "Compact," and was in constant pain from spinal trouble in the neck. She had been wearing a collar for eight months. In spite of devoted medical care, she was gradually losing the power of her right arm and finding it very difficult to lift anything, even her handbag.

She had met a friend casually at the BBC, and it so happened that they had both been invited to a party given by a well-known recording company.

She tells the story herself about the way in which she came to me:

"When my friend announced she was going to take me to a faith healer called Mr. Fricker, I thought she was out of her mind. She told me of her own cure, and I was totally skeptical; but I did not know her well enough to tell her what I thought about this particular kind of nonsense.

"She made an appointment for me and took me to Wyndham Place herself. I felt a complete and utter idiot and also knew how embarrassing it was going to be for everyone when the 'miracle' didn't happen.

"I was not prepared in any way for meeting Ted Fricker. I was expecting a cross between Madame Arcati in *Blithe Spirit* and a famous 'guru' whom I had heard lecture.

"Instead of this, I encountered what appeared to be a perfectly sane-looking man who exuded warmth, friendship, confidence, and great loving-kindness and understanding. Everything in his room was designed to put people off having an imaginary or hysterical healing.

"The room was bright, and cheerful music was playing—totally unlike anything I had expected. I felt even guiltier knowing there was nothing he could do for me.

"I can't explain the feeling of strength and power he is able to transmit through his hands. When he told me to look over my shoulder, I was willing to give it a try, although I didn't have much hope of being able to succeed.

"I can't tell you how it felt when I found that I could move my head, that I could move my arms and there was no pain.

"It was only when the pain went that I fully realized what agony it had been. When an ache creeps up on you a little more each day, you get resigned to it. You take a few more pills so that you can function and continue to work, then more pills to sleep at night, and so it goes on.

"I looked at Ted Fricker in amazement. 'I don't believe in any of this!' I said. He gave me a broad grin and replied, 'I'm the one who has got to believe. Not you.'

"Since then, he has healed three people most dear to me and countless others who had given up hope of a cure and, in some cases, even hope of their lives. Some people feel the way I did when Katie took me to him, but I get them there in spite of themselves.

"I think the most marvelous thing he has given to me is a lack of fear of disease or death, or, even worse, a living death. It doesn't matter, when you go to see him, what type of God you believe in, or indeed if you believe in anything. *He* believes, and *his* understanding is able, thank God, to help us.

"He is a very rare and special person, and I will always be grateful not only for my healing but for the fact that I was able to meet him."

Frances Bennett came to me on December 22, 1964,

which happened to be her own birthday. So she, too, received a kind of surprise birthday gift in the form of an instantaneous cure.

I had another patient, Christopher Lee, who is almost as well known as captain of the team of British celebrity golfers in their matches on television against an American team as he is for his spine-chilling portrayal of Count Dracula.

Here is his account of the healing he received through me:

"I have known Ted Fricker for some years, and I have been to him on several occasions. His faith and his humility, together with the undoubted power that he possesses for the healing of both mind and body, are so well known to countless people who have received at his hands a relief from their pain and unhappiness that it has certainly convinced me that he is one among a chosen few whose mission in life is to help and give succor to those in distress.

"These powers are indeed a gift from God. Ted Fricker himself has always claimed that he is only the instrument, the 'channel.' Whatever the case, healers throughout the ages have achieved miraculous results through the 'laying on of hands,' and this is literally true in the case of Fricker.

"I feel that the process of healing must come from without and within; that is to say, the faith and belief involved do not stem only from the healer but also from those who are healed. In a sense, therefore, one contributes to one's own recovery.

"But to be the catalyst between the source of healing and the result thereof is given to very few. Ted Fricker possesses this gift in abundance, and there are thousands of people in the world today who unquestionably bless his name.

"It is a phenomenon which I personally cannot explain; indeed, few can. But I know from my own experience that Fricker can literally tell you what is wrong with you without any previous knowledge of your condition or any other information.

"His diagnoses are uncanny; his achievements miraculous. There are no other words for it."

Jan Holden, the well-known actress who has been seen so often on television, was obliged to come to me as an emergency case a few years ago.

At the time she was living in the country, and it was her habit when doing a television program to stay in London on the night of the camera rehearsal.

On one such occasion she awoke on the morning of the day when the transmission of the program was to take place and found that she had an acute pain from her head down her spine and in both arms. She could hardly get dressed, and it was quite obvious to her that she was in no condition to give a television performance on that day.

In desperation she took a taxi to my clinic at Wyndham Place, only to find on arrival that the door was locked and nobody was there.

The pain by then was excruciating, but she managed to reach the television studio and she went to the first-aid department.

The nurse sent for the television director, and they both suggested that she should consult the doctor. But she insisted that they telephone and ask me if I could see her. This I agreed to do if she was able to get back to Wyndham Place immediately.

The young producer accompanied her, and it was clear to him that she was convinced that if she could get to "Ted" all would be well.

Let her take up the story herself:

"Ted took me into his room, immediately diagnosed a slipped disc in my neck, and started to 'work.' I felt the power of his hands and the heat on my neck as the cure was taking place.

"Within a few minutes the pain had gone, and Ted explained that the discomfort I then felt was caused by muscles that had been damaged.

"The television producer was astonished when I walked out of the room and said that I was now able to go back to the studio and work.

"The members of the cast could hardly believe that I was able to return and carry on throughout the day, having seen the state I was in two hours earlier.

"Since that time I have had no recurrence of a slipped disc, and once again thank Ted and his 'Guide' for the tremendous help they gave me."

Another famous star of stage and screen who came to see me several years ago was Ann Todd. She was not one of the many patients sent to me by Katie Boyle, but she heard about me in the most unexpected way.

In Brighton seventeen years ago she was set upon and beaten up by thugs in the most shocking way. They left her unconscious on the pavement with damage to the face and jaw which remained for several years until at last the doctor decided that the only thing to do was to operate.

Two weeks before the operation, she was in a taxi on her way to the doctor for a checkup when the taxi driver, without turning his head, said to her, "Don't have an operation! Trust me. Please go and see a wonderful healer!"

There and then, he gave her my address.

She did not delay, and came to see me at the first opportunity. I am happy to say that she was completely cured, and there was no further need for an operation.

In her own words, Ann Todd says:

"It is fascinating, I think, how God works. One's destiny all fits in like a jigsaw puzzle.

"It is a great experience to meet a healer like Ted Fricker. Ted always seems to me to have the strength and power of the universe behind him. He seems to lift one out of one's troubles, and his healing center is a happy place and full of light.

"One thanks God that he has been chosen to help so many, many people."

Ann Todd's meeting with the taxi driver is another example of the mysterious and yet definite way in which people in need of healing are guided to me.

Florence Desmond, the famous actress, came to me sometime ago with severe pain running from the base of her head and down her neck.

She had suffered this affliction for many weeks and had visited several specialists. All had done their best for her but to no avail. She was advised to wear a neck collar. Then traction was tried and heat treatment was given. Nothing helped.

This is how she describes her visit to me:

"My friend Evelyn Laye asked me to visit Mr. Fricker, a faith healer. I said I would go to an Indian witch doctor if it would cure the excruciating pain!

"She took me to Mr. Fricker, and after six treatments of vibration and friction with his hands I was completely cured.

"I don't claim to understand the powers Mr. Fricker possesses. I only know that the result was a complete cure."

Mrs. Mat Munro, wife of the internationally famous singer, had suffered for some years from disc trouble in her back.

This gradually became so serious that it was an intolerable disability for the wife of a singing star who had to travel all over the world.

There came a day when she and her husband were due to fly to Las Vegas, but she was in such pain that it seemed impossible for her to undertake the journey.

Her mother had been one of my patients, but Mrs. Munro herself did not believe in the power of healing. Her husband, on the other hand, was very interested in its possibilities, and on the morning of the day they were to fly to Las Vegas she made up her mind to see me.

I gave her healing, and she was delighted to find that she became well enough to travel, and that evening they boarded the plane.

She feel asleep and the next thing she knew was that they were in Los Angeles. It was quite a time after getting off the plane before she realized that she was walking normally and that her pain had gone.

When they had seen me in London, Mat Munro was very worried and asked me what he should do if his wife's pain should return.

I advised him that the best thing he could do would be to put his hands on her and concentrate on me, and in this way she would receive healing.

He wanted very much to help people, and when he arrived home he tried laying his hands on his family and friends if they were sick. To his surprise the result was very successful.

So in this case not only was someone guided to me who was in need of help, but her husband discovered that he himself could give healing to others.

One Sunday a few years ago I received a telephone call from an agent of Tom Jones, the famous singer. This agent knew me quite well and he said to me, "Ted, will you do me a favor? Tom Jones has just come back from up north, and his voice has gone completely. He has two shows to do today at the London Palladium, and we don't know what to do about it because the theater is fully booked. Could you possibly come down and see him now?"

I told him that I was very sorry but it was my invariable rule not to work on Sundays. He was disappointed, but evidently he made a telephone call to a woman friend who also happened to be a great friend of mine, for a few minutes later she rang me up.

She begged me to go and see Tom Jones, and I felt that I could not refuse her plea.

When the agent telephoned me again at her suggestion, I agreed to go down and see what I could do.

Having arrived at the stage door of the Palladium, I asked for Tom Jones, and after a minute or two the agent came out to talk to me. I had to wait until the doctor who was examining Tom Jones had left, and I was then shown into his dressing room.

It was quite clear that the singer had completely lost his voice, so I started to treat him at once.

After a little while I was told to tell him that his voice was starting to come back, but that when he went on the stage he would find difficulty with the first song. After that, his voice would become quite normal.

He said that he thought he would be able to get through the first song satisfactorily as his first appearance was always greeted by the audience with flowers and other gifts thrown onto the stage amid a great deal of loud applause.

When his call came, he said to me hospitably, "Look, if you would like a drink, there's champagne in the fridge."

However, the agent invited me to go into the auditorium, which I did, and at the same time I concentrated healing thoughts upon the singer.

Things turned out exactly as I had been told. He got through the first song all right and then went on to complete the program with his usual success.

When it was over I went back to his dressing room and gave him some more treatment. I told the agent that the singer's voice should now be quite normal. As I was about to leave, the agent told me that Tom Jones usually went outside during the interval to talk to the hordes of his fans and to sign autographs.

I said that I would not advise him to go out on this occasion and that it would be much better for him to rest before the second performance. So the agent asked me if I would accompany him while he told the fans that Tom Jones had been advised by the doctor to rest.

I readily agreed, not realizing the possible consequences. When we confronted the frustrated crowd of fans and broke the news, the reaction was so unfavorable that I felt I would be lucky to escape all in one piece!

The woman friend who had rung me up attended the second performance that evening and said that she and her companions considered that Tom Jones had never sung better in his life.

I had not met Tom Jones until that day, and afterward I was glad that I had gone to his assistance in spite of its being Sunday, for he is without doubt one of the nicest people it has been my good fortune to come across.

In 1963 Dave Clark, the well-known entertainer, came to see me for the treatment of a growth on the back of his neck. It was arranged that the following week he was to have it removed by surgery. He was in great pain, and in response to the constant urging of his friends, and in desperation, he finally came to me to try and get some relief.

As so many patients do, he frankly told me that he had no faith in healing, but as he had nothing to lose he was prepared to try it.

I laid my hands on the growth and treated it, and after a short while he left, still quite unconvinced. However, this attitude did not last long, for three days later the growth disappeared, leaving no trace. The operation was now completely unnecessary, and his doctor was unable to believe his eyes.

Later on, Dave Clark returned to thank me. I never make predictions of any kind, but on this occasion I made an exception because I thought it would put him in a happy frame of mind. I told him that within a year he would have a record at the top of the list and would receive an engagement at the London Palladium, both of which events came to pass.

Since then, he has sent me a lot of patients. One was a carpenter who was helping to fix up Dave Clark's new penthouse. He fell off a ladder and slipped a disc, and Dave Clark brought him to me. I treated him, and he was able to get back on his ladder the very next day!

On another occasion I had a patient, Lucas Ralli, a well-known figure in the world of business. In 1949 his neck was broken in a car accident, and for months he was encased in plaster.

He traveled to India, where he spent a considerable time in the study of Yoga, and during this period he suffered serious spinal trouble arising from slipped discs.

When he returned to England he came to see me, and I treated his spine. After only a few minutes he was able to go away completely cured.

While I was treating him I realized that he had the power of healing, and I told him of this—as I always do, for God's gift is there to be used in the service of others.

In 1965 he made his first attempt to use his power on a patient by absent healing, and to his amazement he found that it worked. Since then, he has continued to help many people.

He specializes in cases of anxiety, for he believes that this is the cause of much physical illness.

Just as he has been successful in the field of business, so he has used his gift of healing to great effect in the relief of suffering.

Lady Freyberg describes her own experience of an instantaneous cure after many years of suffering:

"Have you ever had a serious physical affliction? Are you now all right, or do you still live with it?

"For twenty years I had two slipped discs, ever-increasing pain, and no one seemed able to help me. I could never stand up straight when I got out of bed in the morning. Eventually the pain became such that I was willing to try anything new.

"A friend suggested that I should go and see Mr. Fricker, of whom I knew little at the time. I went with hope but not much confidence. I was therefore totally unprepared for the instantaneous cure he achieved. Looking back now, all I can say is how wonderful it was to be without constant pain again after so many years of it.

"Since that time, I have introduced many people to Mr. Fricker, and I have been deeply impressed by his extraordinary knowledge and his ability to help with so many difficult problems. Healing is his vocation in life, and he combines it with great kindness and wisdom."

Some years ago when my clinic was still in Tottenham I had a patient who was well known in the business world of the City of London. He suffered from spinal trouble, of which he was cured after I gave him healing. He was a charming man, and when he came to my clinic he used to cheer up all my patients with his friendly chatter.

We became friends, and every now and then he used to telephone me and it was always on a Friday. "You're coming to lunch with me tomorrow, Ted!" he used to say, and I could never refuse him.

He was a most generous host and would take me to an excellent restaurant where we used to chat and laugh together as he liked nothing better than a good joke. We continued to meet after I moved to Wyndham Place.

It was his invariable habit to telephone on a Friday, until one day my secretary came to tell me that he had left a message inviting me to lunch with him on a date six weeks ahead. This date turned out to be a Wednesday, which I instituted as my free day after I moved to Wyndham Place. He had never been there, so he did not, in fact, know this.

It seemed to me so extraordinary that he should invite me to lunch on a day in six weeks' time instead of asking me on the spur of the moment that I asked my secretary to check the date. It seemed that there was no mistake, so the invitation was duly noted in my diary.

When the day arrived he telephoned me and asked, "Shall I pick you up in my car, Ted?"

"Don't trouble," I said, "I'll come down in my own car and meet you at the restaurant. By the way, where are we going?"

"The Mirabelle," he answered. "I'll see you there at one."

Punctually at one o'clock I arrived at the restaurant and found him waiting to greet me.

He gave me the most marvelous lunch, which was accompanied by the telling of many jokes punctuated by much merriment and an occasional friendly pat on the back. It was a happy and memorable meeting, and we did not leave until three o'clock.

He was a big man, and as he stepped into his car he called over his shoulder, "Cheerio, Ted. We'll get together again soon. I'm off to Forest Mere next week to lose several pounds!"

As he shouted this, my Voice suddenly broke in: "He will never go to Forest Mere." I waited for an explanation, but none was forthcoming. The next day I picked up the evening newspaper and read of his death from a heart attack only a few hours after he left me. He was happy when he went, and he never knew anything about it.

Then I realized the reason for his six weeks' invitation to lunch. In the other world it was foreseen that his time to pass on was approaching. He had lived a good life helping people and doing much voluntary work, particularly with regard to youth clubs, and they wanted his passing to be peaceful. To this end, they had put the thought into his mind to invite me to lunch, during which I had touched him several times with a friendly slap on the back. This had the effect of putting in sufficient power to loosen the silver cord joining his spirit to his body so that his passing was made more swiftly and easily.

He was a good friend, and I was happy to have been allowed to perform this last service for him.

As I write these words in January 1976, my telephone has not stopped ringing for days with requests for help from people who have a relative who has just suffered a heart attack. In my twenty-five years of healing I have never known so many people to be attacked by this illness in a matter of weeks.

When someone passes the age of forty, this illness becomes more likely to happen to him. But it can be avoided.

As the arteries get older they require oil, and if they do not get this, they tend to dry up and wither. This can cause the blood to clot in the arteries, and then the heart stops beating.

The way to avoid this is have a massage with baby oil once a week. But if you cannot afford this, then baby oil should be rubbed into the skin before getting into the bath. As the hot water opens the pores of the skin, so the oil will soak into the body and will eventually reach the arteries. This will give the arteries greater elasticity and will help to keep them free from blood clots.

11

How We Can Heal Each Other

There is another and very important question which I am very often asked: "Can you cure cancer?"

This is quite understandable since as yet no cure has been discovered by medical science.

The only treatments which in some cases have proved successful are both destructive—surgery and the use of powerful rays which can be effective but by which tissues are destroyed irrevocably.

I have cured many cases of cancer, but where it has been treated with rays it is very difficult and sometimes impossible for me to do anything about it. It all depends how much tissue has been destroyed, and if too much damage has been done, then a cure is out of the question.

As I have already explained, the tissues of the body are like batteries, and if a large part of them has been burned away, there is then nothing for me to recharge with healing power. I know that in many cases which come under medical care there seems to be no alternative to ray treatment.

If the treatment is not successful and there is a recurrence of the cancer, then it is too late for me to help in cases where too much tissue has been destroyed.

But if the doctors before taking this drastic step would let a healer treat a patient, there would be a good chance that the cancer would be cured.

When we are sick, the healing power within our own tissues is used up more quickly in combating the illness, and therefore we require more frequent recharging. Often when patients are very ill, doctors forbid them visitors, which is a mistake, for it is just at this time that they require more recharging by others touching them. However, if no visitors are allowed, the nurse can do a great deal to recharge the patient with power simply by holding his hand.

There are, of course, some cases where the patient's time to leave this world is near, and this cannot be altered. But in many cancer cases this is not so, and the healing power can remove the disease and give the patient an extended span of happy life.

Only a short time ago a young woman in her late thirties came to see me with severe migraine, from which she recovered after I gave her healing.

"You don't remember me, do you, Mr. Fricker?" she said.

I confessed that I did not.

"Fourteen years ago I came to you with cancer after I had been given only a few days to live, and you cured me," she reminded me.

Then I recalled the case, which was reported in a newspaper at the time. She told me that since then she had had no trace of cancer and had lived a normal happy life.

Another case I treated a few years ago was that of a businessman who had cancer of the lip.

It had been treated by the use of rays, and although not painful at the time, it shortly afterward developed into a festering sore which made eating a problem, and drinking had to be done through a straw. The pain became almost unbearable.

"My wife implored me to visit Ted Fricker," he says, "who, seeing me on a Thursday, announced after treatment that I would be totally cured by the following Monday.

"At the time this remark seemed impossible to believe, but from that moment onward relief started, and by the morning in question there was a complete healing of the sore, and pain had gone.

"It is just another small testimony of the healing power of this truly remarkable man to whom the Almighty has given such a gift."

Fortunately in this case not too much tissue had been destroyed by the ray treatment, and healing was still possible.

These are only two cases of many where it was not necessary for people in the prime of life to die of this terrible disease.

During the last fifty years a superficial medical knowledge has become widely disseminated among the lay public, which in many ways is unfortunate.

People almost demand of their doctor that he should tell them all about their illness. I do not think this is a good thing at all because it is much better for a person—provided he observes the normal rules of personal hygiene and takes care not to abuse his body—to think as little about illness as possible and leave it to the doctor to treat him.

If a patient is told too much about his illness, he tends to worry about it, and by concentrating his mind upon it, the condition can be greatly aggravated.

When I started healing, my Voice explained to me the

way in which the mind can affect the body, and I was told that I must learn from personal experience.

I was instructed to sit down and imagine that I had a pain in my knee and to concentrate my mind upon it. I did as I was told and focused my thoughts for half an hour on one of my knees until I was told to get up from my chair. I did so, and promptly fell flat on my face as my knee was temporarily crippled.

Everybody without exception is afraid of cancer, and if they are told that they have the disease, then the tendency is for the mind to become fixed upon it in acute anxiety, which has the effect of aggravating the condition. I cannot see that any good is achieved by telling a patient. A great deal of harm may be done, and great distress caused.

Honey and water are two of nature's medicines, and honey—if taken regularly—can be effective in the prevention of cancer by supplying all parts of the body with the vital substances which are necessary. Also, if cancer is suspected, honey can help build up the body's resistance and assist in the cure.

It is much better to keep our minds off the subject of illness altogether. Every morning we should awaken to the new day as though we had just been born. We should try to cultivate a state of mind which is free of anxiety, regardless of the bad news and adverse weather reports. How often have we worried ourselves sick about things which, in fact, never happened? Somehow, troubles have a way of sorting themselves out in the end, and we should try and remember this even if the sky seems overcast at the moment. Let us try and live only for the day in a state of hope, faith, and love, casting out fear altogether from our minds.

Sufficient unto the day is the evil thereof.

When they are in trouble, most people pray to God for

help—more in hope than in faith that there is a God. I know that God exists, and my greatest wish is to convince everyone that not only does God exist but that He is fully aware of every small detail of our daily problems. We should pray to Him, and if it is His Will, our prayer will be answered, sometimes in the way we least expect.

Make your prayer once only to God, and then leave it all to Him and you will find that He will often guide you to someone who will be able to provide a solution.

Many clergymen have been among my patients, but I must confess that I was never a great churchgoer, although as most people do, I used to go on special occasions.

When I first started healing, I asked my Voice if it was necessary for me to become more religious than I had been up to that time. I was told that the religion that I was to follow was God's Law that we should love one another and help each other, not necessarily with money but with kind words of loving encouragement—and in my particular case by using my gift of healing.

All the great religions are manifestations of God's Word, and all those who practice them are God's children. If it gives them comfort to go to church or temple, this can do nothing but good.

Although they suffered severe persecution, the early Christians were happy people, and I always feel that religion should be joyful. When I am healing the sick, I have with me six doctors who come from the Christ sphere in the other world, and they laugh and joke with me all day long.

I see every day among my patients the effect that laughter and cheerfulness can produce.

When new patients come to me, they are very often apprehensive because they are not sure what is going to happen.

My elder daughter, Rita, was my first receptionist and was followed later by her younger sister, Theresa, who is with me now. Both of them have been blessed with happy natures and the ability to converse easily with people and put them at their ease.

Thanks to them, my waiting room has always been a happy place, and often when I come in there I am greeted by laughter and cheerful conversation not only with Theresa but also among the patients themselves. Such has been the happy influence of my two daughters that my patients come into my consulting room already half-cured!

When some more serious illness attacks you, and your batteries have become very run down, then you are guided to someone who is a born healer like myself.

When I give healing to people, I am advised by doctors in the other world who were specialists on this earth either in heart disease or arthritis and so on. When they reach the other world, their abilities increase because they can see in advance what is likely to happen.

If I am treating a person for heart trouble, the heart doctor tells me where to put my hands, how long to hold them there, and when to take them away, because this power that comes through my body is so strong.

During healing I can hear the doctor advising me, and as my hands are guided to the affected part, healing takes place.

I do not let my material mind interfere in any way, because I am only the instrument, and God's power works through me. I have to keep my thoughts entirely away from what I am doing so that I can allow myself to be guided from the other world.

It is not necessary for a patient to have any faith at all when he comes to see me. He may be the biggest disbeliever in the world. It is not he who has to have faith;

it is I who have to do so, and this is why I call myself a faith healer.

I have to have faith to do what I am told to do and to repeat what I am told to tell him.

Sometimes a paralyzed person may come to me, and I am told that before I touch him I must tell him that I am going to cure him. I am warned that if I do not tell him, then he will not be cured. And so I have to have sufficient faith to tell him.

There are many people who would like to come to me for healing but who are prevented from doing so because they live too far away or are tied by their personal obligations.

In fact, this need not prevent them from receiving healing, even if they only know of me by name. If a person were to sit down for half an hour in a chair once a day, concentrate his thoughts on my name, and ask for my help, he would be able to establish contact and draw power from me in this way. This can take place in seconds, wherever you my live in the world. It would certainly help him, and might even cure him.

He would find that a deep calmness would come to him. He might experience a tingling sensation around his body, and sometimes might be conscious of the perfume of carnations. The carnation is my spiritual flower.

Thousands of people all over the world—whom I would not know if I were to meet them—concentrate on me in this way and receive benefit. I have frequently received letters from them telling me that they have experienced the scent of this beautiful perfume of carnations while they have been trying to make contact with me. But it must be remembered that it is of no use to sit down and concentrate just for the sake of experiencing the scent of carnations.

Only a few weeks ago I was explaining to a woman patient how to go about this absent healing. She asked me how she would know when she had made contact with me, and I told her that besides the feeling of calmness which would come to her, she might be conscious of the scent of carnations.

She came back to me about a fortnight later and told me how she had been trying to carry out my instructions about absent healing. It appeared that on the evening of the very day that I had last seen her, she had given a dinner party. As she had finished her dressing half an hour before her husband was ready, she thought she would fill in the interval before her guests arrived by trying out what I had told her. So she sat down in a chair, tried to relax, and spent the next half hour sniffing expectantly without any result. No scent of carnations rewarded her efforts.

Her concentration was interrupted by the sound of the doorbell announcing the arrival of some of her guests. When she opened the door she found four people on the doorstep, and before she had time to greet them they all exclaimed, "What a wonderful scent of carnations. You must have the house full of them!"

"I haven't a carnation in the place," she said.

Having shown her guests into the lounge, she went to fetch her husband, and as he descended the stairs he called to her, "I can smell the scent of carnations! Did they bring you some as a present?"

By this time his wife was thoroughly upset because she could smell absolutely nothing at all!

This is a classic example of what happens if you try to demand to order something from the other world. Because this woman had done this by concentrating only on the perfume, her demand had blocked the channel by which it would have come. You cannot demand anything from the other world, for it only comes as a free gift from those who wish to bestow it.

Exactly the same rule applies to the act of prayer.

Even as a child I was told by my Voice that if I wished to pray for anything at all, then I must ask God only once. After making my request I must put the whole thing out of my mind, and if God decided to grant what I had asked, one day I would receive it when I least expected it. I have learned that God loves to surprise you just as a father loves to surprise his child. The prayer must not be in set form but must come straight from the heart in simple words.

We must not bother God by praying for the same thing every night because this will create a block.

If it were not so, we should tend to become too arrogant and demanding, considering that we have a right to have all our requests granted. Such is human nature. Our attitude of mind must be one of humility, as a child speaking to a father, grateful for any gift which it may be His Will to send to us.

There is nothing for which you cannot pray to God. Your prayer may be for others or for your family or even about your business affairs. But the rule is that the prayer must come sincerely from your heart and that you must ask only once. Then you must forget it and be prepared to accept whatever gift God may send in His own good time. This is the way to pray.

In 1970 I had a very serious case of spinal trouble in the person of a woman who had a really appalling history of pain and illness which had continued incessantly for about eight years.

In 1962 she had developed pains in her back which

gradually worsened until she was driven to seek medical advice. The doctor said that she had a slipped disc, for which a steel support was prescribed. Day and night for five years she wore it, and she still bears the scars where the support had dug deep into her skin. There was no change for the better. After all this time she was told that nothing further could be done and that she would have to learn to "live with it."

The poor woman was in such a state that her husband felt that he must try to do something, and so he decided to make an appointment for her to see an osteopath.

After a year's treatment there was no improvement, but owing to the fact that her husband had been made redundant she was forced to go out to work.

One of her colleagues at work told her of another manipulator, and she felt that perhaps the treatment might do her some good. But once again she was disappointed.

She had "lived with it" now for seven years, and there was no doubt that her condition was deteriorating. And so she stopped all treatment and resigned herself to a life of suffering and the probability of ending up in a wheelchair.

In the spring of 1970 she began to have terrible pain in her arms and across her shoulders whenever she went to bed, and in order to get some relief, her husband had to massage her arms several times during the night, which proved a most exhausting procedure. During one week she was given fourteen different types of tablets, none of which made any difference.

By this time her husband was at his wits' end and in desperation arranged for her to go once more into the hospital.

She was given a number of tests, including a lumbar puncture. Her husband was told that she was suffering from high blood pressure, osteoarthritis, a slipped disc, and that she was mentally and physically run down, and for good measure that she was also overweight.

She was advised to take a holiday away from everything. She acted on this advice, and the whole family went for a holiday to Newquay.

There she got into conversation with an acquaintance of several years' standing who said that her own husband had been cured of a duodenal ulcer by a Mr. Fricker in London. The husband confirmed this and was so convinced by the healing he had received at my hands that he announced himself willing to pay all the expenses incurred if she was not cured.

Immediately on returning home, her husband wrote to my clinic for an appointment. As the list was very full and no cancellations were available, I wrote a letter promising to give her absent healing and suggesting that she should concentrate on me at nine o'clock each evening.

It so happened that on the evening of the same day when she received my letter, it had been arranged that she and her husband were to visit the theater. The interval between the acts occurred at exactly nine o'clock, and while her husband was getting a drink she settled herself down in a corner and taking out my letter she began to concentrate on my photograph at the top of the notepaper.

"It was the most eerie sensation," she wrote. "My legs tingled, and I felt 'distant.' This lasted for about ten minutes and then passed. What I expected, I have no idea, but nothing else seemed to have happened and I went to bed as usual."

The next morning she awoke and, without thinking, she just turned over. Then it suddenly struck her that this was something she had been unable to do for years without very severe pain and great effort. In tremendous excitement she called to her husband and showed him so many times how she could roll back and forth that he became quite alarmed.

Not only that, but she got out of bed unassisted and raised her left leg without effort to put on her stocking—the same leg which for two years she had not been able to lift higher than an inch or two.

"From that day to this," she asserted, "I have dressed without assistance, whereas for years I needed some help if I bent down for any reason."

A week before Christmas 1970, an appointment was made and she came to see me.

"Two visits and all was well with my back and shoulders," she said. "I felt fit again. It was unbelievable."

During 1973 her arthritis became troublesome, and without delay she came to see me again. After a few treatments her pain disappeared and she was able to get about quite normally.

"No words of mine can express my gratitude to Mr. Fricker for all he has done for me," she finished.

"Don't thank me, my dear," I told her. "Thank God."

I am like a power station through which God's healing power flows. If a person is sick, all he has to do is to concentrate his thoughts for half an hour each day upon me—the power station whom he may never have seen. It is sufficient if he knows me only by name. If he then asks for help, he will receive it.

This daily contact must be religiously observed until such time as sufficient alleviation or a cure has been brought about, and it must be done sincerely.

If a child is sick, the parent can lay hands on the child's head or body and at the same time concentrate upon me by name, asking for help for the afflicted child.

Preferably the hands should be placed on each side of the affected part of the body, but if this for some reason is not possible, then the hands can be put on each side of the head, or in the last resort both the hands of the child can be held.

This should be done for two or three minutes at a time and as often as possible.

The following story serves as an excellent example of the effectiveness of the transmission of healing power to a patient through the laying on of hands by another person.

I now call it the case of the "Running Child." The reason for this will become apparent toward the end of the story.

About six months ago a former patient, the sculptress who had made the bronze head which stands in my consulting room, telephoned me to ask if I could help the child of a friend of hers who was desperately ill. I asked her to send the father to visit me and I would see if anything could be done.

An appointment was made, and when he arrived it appeared that the situation was much more serious than I had expected. He told me that the little boy, Marcus, had developed a very sore throat and had been treated by the doctor for tonsillitis. But after a week he got much worse, and the doctor realized that it was not tonsillitis and suspected that it was meningitis or encephalitis. He was admitted to a hospital immediately, and within two days he was paralyzed and was undergoing fits and seizures. Drugs had no effect, and his condition continued to deteriorate until within a short time the poor child—in his father's words—"was like a cabbage."

The neurologist had to tell the child's mother that the

chance of his recovery was one in a hundred, but later in the evening of that day the unhappy parents received the news that there was no hope at all.

The father was stunned, and since no purpose would be served by his waiting about at the hospital, he left in order to fulfill an engagement at the Royal Academy, for he himself was a sculptor by profession.

It was at the door of the Royal Academy that he unexpectedly met my former patient, the sculptress, and having listened to his tragic story, she advised him to come and see me, which he did as soon as he was able to fix an appointment.

He asked me if I would come to the hospital and treat the child, but regretfully I had to tell him that pressure of work rendered this impossible. His disappointment was obvious, but I said to him, "Don't give up hope, because if you do exactly as I tell you, I will treat the child by using your hands to give him healing, and this can be just as effective as though I were to treat him in person."

I told him to visit the hospital as often as possible and to lay his hands upon the boy's head and at the same time to keep the thought of me in his mind with the maximum of concentration. I then asked him to telephone me at intervals and report how the child was responding to treatment.

Immediately the father went straight to the hospital and did exactly as I had told him. Within a day or two there was a slight improvement, and when he let me know, I told him to continue religiously with my instructions.

In spite of the change for the better, the doctors were not very encouraging in their prognosis and told the father that from their experience in such cases it was certain that the child would be physically disabled and mentally retarded, however much his condition seemed to improve. They also said that the child's left arm would be paralyzed.

In spite of this gloomy prediction, the father persisted in his treatment of the boy and never wavered for an instant, and the left arm started to get better.

The next day he returned to the hospital, only to be told the news that his son was blind, deaf, and dumb. In order to satisfy himself that this was really so, that evening the father walked into the child's room as noisily as possible and waved his arms in front of the boy's eyes. There could be no doubt that his son was deaf and blind. But the father did not give up his effort and again put his hands upon the child's head.

The next morning he returned early to the hospital and gave his son breakfast. Hoping desperately for some sign of change, the father held up the child's toy in front of his eyes.

The result was electrifying. The child suddenly grabbed the toy out of his father's hand, in spite of the fact that he was so weak. The seemingly impossible had happened. His son could see and hear once more.

Week by week a steady progress was maintained until at the end of a month the child was discharged from the hospital and allowed to return home.

The doctors thought that the illness was probably encephalitis and that whatever damage remained would be permanent. They did a test on the boy which is normally done only on adults and discovered there was a lesion on the brain stem, so that there was no coordination at all.

When he left the hospital, the child was not fully recovered. He was not able to walk at all as there was still a partial paralysis.

I told the father to continue to lay his hands on the

child at home. Within another month he was almost completely cured, and then on January 2, 1976, the father brought the child to see me for the first time. The little boy ran into my consulting room, and after examination I was able to confirm that a complete cure had taken place.

The father had brought me a gift in the form of the most beautiful sculpture which he had named "Running Child." It expresses all the vigor and joyous movement of a child in perfect health and will always serve to remind me of the happiness and satisfaction I experienced from the child's recovery.

I never saw the boy until that day and had seen the father only on the first occasion.

To my mind it is a classic example of this method of healing, and I am glad that the father had the faith and the will to carry out my instructions, so that God's healing power was transferred from me to the child through the father's own hands.

I have already said that some of the most extraordinary things that have happened in my life have taken place near Christmastime.

The final healing of this child was one of the most wonderful experiences I have ever had, and it happened on the eighth day of Christmas.

The same procedure can be adopted with an adult who is too ill to concentrate by himself. This physical contact is essential where the patient is being treated by another person, and power can only be transmitted in this way. But it must be stressed that the hands must never be laid on without concentrating on the healer; otherwise, the power of the one who is trying to help will be drained away from him into the body of the sick patient. Someone who is ill uses up power much more quickly than a healthy person.

It can be done by doctors and nurses in hospitals in exactly the same manner. When the hands are laid upon the patient and the concentration is fixed upon my name, power will begin to flow through me to the patient by way of the hands of the doctor or nurse. At the same time, one of my doctors or helpers in the other world will come and stand beside the one whose hands are upon the patient and will try to guide him to put his hands in the right place and to do what is best for the one who is ill.

Sometimes, if the patient is not too ill, the healing power can be increased by a person laying his hands on the patient and concentrating on me while the patient himself at the same time concentrates his own thoughts on me as well.

Anyone can perform this service of healing for a sick person, provided it is done with the utmost sincerity. And in the laying of hands upon another who is ill we are obeying the injunction of Christ that we should love and help one another.

The month of March—as well as the Christmas season—has always been a very fortunate time in my life when pleasant things seem to happen. March 1976 proved to be no exception.

I was treating one of my patients at Wyndham Place on March 2, when she happened to mention that a woman friend of hers had just undergone a very serious operation for the removal of a brain tumor.

Although the operation had been successful, it appeared that unforeseen complications had set it, and I therefore suggested that she could receive healing if her husband were to lay his own hands upon her and think of me.

The operation to remove the brain tumor had been

successfully performed on February 27, but unfortunately the next day a clot of blood formed which necessitated a second operation. This went well, and it was hoped that all would be plain sailing. However, it was not to be, and on February 29 it was found that fluid was pressing on the brain, causing fits of an epileptic nature.

I had given my patient instructions to the husband as to the way the hands should be placed for healing, together with my photograph as an aid to concentration.

These were delivered to him on March 3, and he went at the earliest opportunity to the hospital to see his wife. It was too difficult for him to lay his hands on her head, and so he simply held both her hands in his and concentrated on my photograph asking for help according to my instructions.

She was having alternating bouts of consciousness and unconsciousness, and on March 4 her condition reached a state of crisis. The next day she was put on a respirator in the hope of dispersing the fluid by an increased supply of oxygen. The surgeon was very concerned and said that if there was no improvement in her condition within forty-eight hours he feared that her chances of recovery were slim.

Meanwhile, the husand continued to treat her constantly by holding her hands, and by eleven in the evening there was some sign of improvement.

That night the husband stayed close to the hospital with his daughter, but sleep was not possible. At five o'clock in the morning on March 6 he was lying awake in bed when he quite distinctly heard a distant Voice saying, "She will get better, but it will take time."

His reaction, he says, was not one of incredulity. He accepted what the Voice had said without question, and he felt the great weight of fear and anxiety lifted from him.

The feeling was so strong that he noted the time. A wonderful feeling of calm descended upon his mind, and he turned over and immediately fell into an untroubled sleep.

At eight-thirty A.M. he awoke and telephoned the hospital. The cheerful voice of the nurse in the intensive-care ward answered him with the news that his wife had taken a definite turn for the better—at five in the morning.

She was kept on the respirator for a further twenty-four hours, and on the morning of March 8 she was allowed to return to her own room.

The partial paralysis of the left arm is getting better, and she is now able to walk unassisted. Her condition is improving daily, and the prognosis is a happy one. At my suggestion, her husband is continuing to treat her, which is essential until her recovery is complete.

On the morning of March 6 when the crisis had passed, the husband went to see the surgeon, for whose skill and unremitting care and concern as well as that of the nurses he has the deepest gratitude. He told him about the healing treatment he was giving to his wife, and to his surprise the surgeon showed not the slightest trace of skepticism.

This case is a good example of the way in which absent healing can be used to help a sick adult, and can also be employed in conjunction with medical treatment.

But there is more to it than that. The wife, who did not believe in healing, is now convinced of its truth. She has experienced the same feeling of calmness and peace of mind as her husband, who says that his faith in God has been renewed and his whole outlook on life has been changed.

Their happiness is my reward, and it gives me a deep satisfaction.

God has shown in this way that His divine healing power heals not only the body but also the spirit.

It was originally God's intention—so I have been told—that everyone should be able to receive absent healing either through establishing contact with a healer by means of concentration on him directly or through the hands of another who concentrates on the healer.

It is not necessary to visit the healer, and indeed this limits the number of patients who can be treated in any given period—whereas the number who can receive absent healing in the same period is practically limitless.

God has placed a great number of healers all over the world who become known in their particular areas, and thus a network of healing power stations is established which is available to all people on earth.

It is the most wonderful gift that God has bestowed upon mankind, and I would urge those readers who are in doubt to give it a fair trial.

Epilogue

I have traveled far along the road of life, and before I go in the natural way to a new life in the other world, I would like to feel that I have done all in my power to awaken people's minds to the truth of the existence of healing power as a reality of life.

I believe that this was the reason for which I was put on this earth. I cannot do more than tell people about it. After that, they can accept it or reject it as they wish.

Doubters there must be, but I ask them to try and find out the truth about it for themselves and to remember that, in the words of Jesus: "With God, all things are possible."

My most sincere hope is that the writing of this book has given you some understanding of both worlds.

If it only succeeds in bringing help and comfort to those poor souls who are old and alone with nothing they can look forward to but the approach of death, then it has achieved its purpose.

I know that many of you will not find it possible to believe everything you have read in these pages. All that I can say to you is that there will come a time when you will know that what I have written is the truth, and that will be the hour when you are called "home."

At last I have finished the task which I was told to carry out, and this is one of the happiest days of my life.

GOD BLESS YOU ALL!